BEGINNING FAMILY DOG TRAINING

Patricia B. McConnell, Ph.D.

Cover photo by Karen B. London
Cover model: "Molly" American Eskimo,
owned by Aimee Moore.
Cover Design by Sarah Wolstenholme

For information, contact:
Dog's Best Friend, Ltd.
P.O. Box 447
Black Earth, WI 53515
608/767-2435

ISBN 1-891767-03-8

Printed in the United States of America

5 6 7 8 9

Acknowledgments

Special thanks go to Aimee Moore, Dr. Ellen Leiferman, Dr. Calico Schmidt, Dawn Seibel, Rachel Shoshana Klopfer, Karen Stanley, Brenda Scidmore and Karen London, whose comments and advice have done much to improve early versions of this book. Thanks also go to Dmitri Bilgere and Sarah Wolstenholme, for layout, typesetting and generally overall great advice. Denise Swedlund somehow keeps the office running as smoothly as greyhounds in the wind, for which I shall always be indebted.

This book is dedicated to the good dog Drift,
who taught me as much as I was ready to learn.

Contents

Introduction

Congratulations! You are on your way to having a happy, well-behaved dog. By committing time and energy to your dogs' education you have taken the most important step in training—understanding that Lassies are made, not born.

Dogs don't arrive knowing the intricacies of North American society, and they don't come able to read your mind. You have to raise your canine companions to learn what is proper behavior and what is not. And just as your dog doesn't instinctively know what you want, we humans don't necessarily know how to explain it to them. We aren't born knowing how to train dogs, anymore than we inherently know how to be a veterinarian. If you really want a dog who happily does what you ask, you need to understand at least three things:

- the *natural history* of dogs

- how to *communicate* with an individual of another species (it's hard enough within our own species, right?)

- the *basics of learning*—or how to effect another individuals' behavior.

Thus, the goal of this book is to teach you a bit about how dogs *think*, how they *communicate*, and how they *learn*. Mastering dog training and handling is far beyond the scope of this book, or any other for that matter, so think of this book as a starter manual—an introduction for beginners or a reminder of basics for those of you who are more experienced. When reading through this book I encourage you to jot notes, underline, or stop reading and run off to try something out with your dog. Do anything that gets your mind wrapped around the ideas and exercises within each chapter. In other words, try to *learn* what's in these pages, not just read it.

The book is divided into six sections. It was originally designed to supplement Dog's Best Friend's Beginning Family Dog Training Classes, but can also be used by itself to help families get a good start with their dog. If in classes, you will get the most benefit from reading each chapter immediately after training class, and then again the next morning. If working alone, work on each section in depth before moving along to the next.

Think of the next several weeks as training for *all* the family. Get everyone involved so they can all learn to communicate effectively. Imagine trying to learn a new language when everyone in the house spoke a different one! Do everything you can to incorporate these ideas into your daily routine. That means thinking about it enough that it becomes automatic. Remember when you had to think about each little move you made when you learned to drive a car? Now that all comes automatically, because you began by concentrating your attention and practicing a lot. That's what you need to do for the next six weeks, until your behavior becomes a habit. The exact same thing will happen with your dog—weeks of learning some new behavioral patterns will become years of good manners, and doing the right thing will become the *only* thing to do.

And above all, I sincerely hope you and your family and your dog have *fun*. That *is* why you got a dog, right?!

My best wishes go with you,

Patricia McConnell

Chapter 1

Canine Communication

Remember, dogs don't read minds, and they don't come speaking English! To teach them English, *you* must first learn "dog." Many obedience problems are a result of the dog simply not understanding what you want. You are both teacher and translator—it's up to you to help them figure out what you want.

Focus this week on how you try to tell your dog what you want. I find it helpful to be aware of the different ways we can try to influence a dog's behavior.

CHEMICAL (SMELL). Chemical signals are the dog's primary means of exploring the world. Some *favorite* dog smells include rotten fish, fresh cow manure, and bitches in heat. Any of these things would get a dog's attention. Luckily, you can send some very interesting chemical signals without carrying a smelly fish or a lusty Pomeranian in your pocket. Liver, hot dogs, or smelly dog treats are great for getting your dog's attention. Food smells are particularly helpful as a signal to "lure" the dog into a desired posture. For example, puppies can be taught to sit by holding a piece of food no more than a half inch above their nose, and then moving the food back (not up) toward their tail. The action of following this motivating signal causes the dog to raise his head and lower his rump. Bingo! Your dog just sat without you having to force him* to do anything.

Smell allows you to "lure" your dog into almost any position, without pushing, poking or prodding at him. We know from laboratory experiments that animals learn fastest if allowed to initiate an action themselves, rather than being forced (even gently) into it. The key here is to hold the food right by the dog's nose, within a half inch, and slowly move your hand so that the dog's nose follows. If your dog stops following the food with his head, simply move your hand right back to almost touching his nose and begin again. We'll talk more about this as a training tool at the end of the chapter. This technique is called the *"lure/reward"* method.

---

* Since "he or she" is awkward, I'll alternate genders, rather than using "it" when referring to dogs. Consider it neuvo-alternate-biology.

VISUAL. *Dogs primarily use visual signals to communicate with each other. If you learn anything from this book, learn this.* Your dog is watching while you are talking. Of course dogs whine, bark, and occasionally howl, and thus use sound to "talk" to each other on occasion. And all of our dogs *eventually* learn word commands, but my research suggests that visual signals overwhelm sounds if presented simultaneously, so you must be aware of how you are moving your body when you signal your dog. I suspect that this is the most common cause of miscommunication with dogs: you think they respond to your spoken "Sit" when they have actually learned to sit when you tilt your head forward (or move your finger, or raise your arm). The problem is that we usually aren't aware of how our body moves, so we change our visual cues unknowingly from time to time. Our dogs become confused, and eventually learn to ignore us.

Some visual signals don't need to be taught: dogs tend to naturally respond to your squatting or bowing down as if it were the "play bow" of a litter mate, and come running to play. Standing tall and moving abruptly forward has the opposite effect, stopping dogs in their tracks like a traffic cop. So you can use these signals consciously to help your dog do what you want, or you can inadvertently sabotage the message of your signals by saying one thing with your voice and something *completely* different with your body.

Other visuals have to be taught, but dogs appear to learn them very fast, especially if they are linked with the "lure/reward" method mentioned above. For example, use the smell of food in your hand to cause the dog to raise his head, and thus lower his rump. As you move the food toward the dog's tail you are also moving your hand, and thus teaching your dog to "Sit" to that particular hand movement. Teaching "Down" uses the same concept, in that luring the dog's head down toward the ground with food includes moving your hand in a sweeping downward motion. Within a week or two (only days with many dogs) your dog will learn that the motion itself is a signal from you to him. Dogs attend to *movement* particularly (rather than static postures), so make each movement clear and crisp.

"It's not what you say...it's how you say it!"

ACOUSTIC. Although visual signals are critical when communicating with your dog, your *voice* can also have a profound effect on your dog's behavior. For example, canids interpret *pitch* as an important element in the message of the signal—high or squeaky noises are perceived to be excited, friendly and appeasing. On the other hand, low, growly noises are authoritative or inhibiting. Thus, saying "Spot, Come" in a low, loud growl is the perfect way to insure that Spot stays at least ten yards away from you! After all, you just informed him, in dog language, that you're going to bite him if he gets anywhere near you. How dumb is Spot?

And saying "No!" in a high, wavering voice *really* says to your dog "Yes! Wasn't that Fun!! Let's do it again!!!!" or "Gosh, I really don't want you to do that but since you're the leader of the pack, I'm afraid to interfere." Hardly the message that will effectively stop Spot from chewing on the electric cord. So verbal corrections should be low and growly notes, "Come!" should be a bit higher and more animated, and inhibiting signals like "Stay" should be given as low pitched, flat or slowly descending notes ("Staaaaay").

How long or short the word is can also be critical to getting the response you want. Keep most of your acoustic signals relatively *short*—one word is best for your "foundation" word. Careful of giving long lectures like…"No Spot, I told you never to get on the couch, Nonononononowhydon'tyouEVERlistentome?!?" You probably lost Spot somewhere around the third word, and are simply communicating that you are a psycho. He'll just wish you'd go away so he can get on with this great new game of jumping on the couch and chewing on the pillows!

Verbal corrections should be short, abrupt notes, spoken in a low and growly voice. You are trying to elicit a *startle response*, not beat the dog with your voice! On the other hand, stimulating signals like "Come!" should be short, rising in pitch, and rapidly repeated…"Pup, pup, pup" while clapping your hands, or using short, rising whistles. My research found that a series of short, repeated notes *stimulate* movement…so slap your leg, clap your hands, tap the ground, and/or make smooching noises to get that pup *moving!* (Keep in mind that my research didn't predict where they'd go once stimulated, so you still have to teach your dog to come *to you* rather than go chase the cows when you make these noises!) On the other hand, the only time I use long, extended words is when I want to slow down or soothe an animal. I say "Staaaaaaay" or "Gooooooooooooood Dog" when I want to inhibit movement or keep a dog quiet.

Calling your dog to come to you is the perfect example of using (or misusing) both visual and acoustic signals. Call "Spot Come!" and get Spot's attention with hand claps and smooches. Dogs love to chase moving things, so as soon as he looks at you, run away from him as you continue clapping. The instant that he runs toward you repeat "Good Dog!" with lots of "pitch modulation" or up and down notes in your voice. Keep running (visual signal) clapping and praising (acoustical signals), eventually bending down and over in a doggy play bow (visual signal). Compare that with standing straight up, stock still, and belting out a drill sergeant's version of *"Come!"*—Which would *you* come to?

When you give your verbal signal is important, and I'll discuss timing in greater detail throughout the upcoming chapters. But do remember that as with "Come," use the same timing for all signals; say "Sit" as he begins to sit, and "Down" as he starts to lie down…not before or after the movement. This takes some practice, but it's far superior to shouting out a command first, and then making the dog do it.

PHYSICAL. Physical signals are an integral part of pack communication. If you can't bear the idea of ever physically correcting a dog, maybe you should get a cat. This does *not* mean, however, that you should be manhandling your dog, pushing, pulling or jerking at him half of his life. Physical corrections should be given as rarely as possible, and with just enough force to effectively communicate to your dog that he is being corrected. Most of the jerking and slapping and leash pulling that I see people do to their dog should be replaced with either non–physical signals or "remote distraction" corrections, which startle the dog into ceasing and desisting. At that point, you can then redirect their behavior.

"Force is simply the absence of real power, and no matter how gentle, is always the last method to use when controlling your dog."

Try very, *very* hard to get control of your dog's behavior *without* relying on a leash or your hands. Every time you resort to forcing your dog into doing something, you are communicating that you have no real power over the dog, unless you are attached by a leash or grabbing at her with your hands. Force, after all, is simply the absence of real power, and no matter how gentle, is always the last method to use when controlling your dog.

Most of the time you can control your dog's behavior by understanding the effect of your visual signals, and by learning the visual signals that dogs send to each other. We will work extensively on these in later chapters. For now, remember that punishment is the *least* effective way of changing any animal's behavior and is usually more an expression of our impatience than good training techniques. Punishment often simply teaches your dog to be afraid of you, and can result in defensive aggression in return.

Remote Corrections. Sometimes a good alternative to punishment is to use a "remote" signal, or something that stops your dog from misbehaving without you having to run toward him. Throwing an empty pop can with coins in it as you say "No!" startles some dogs just enough so that they stop what they were doing. Be aware, however, that noisy pop cans are too scary for some dogs. In this case, a tossed bean bag or a slap on the wall is all you need. One of these methods should startle your dog into stopping what he is doing and look up. You now have the opportunity to *instantly* redirect him so that he is doing something appropriate rather than mischievous. Don't look for your dog to look terrified, that's not your goal. Even if he goes and picks up the pop can you've just thrown, you still distracted him from what he was doing, and thus your "No" worked!. I use this kind of correction in place of a physical one often, especially for young puppies who don't yet understand what "No!" means.

However, occasionally you simply have to physically correct your dog on some occasions. I most often use a "Body Block" (I'll talk about this more later) that still avoids even touching the dog. In rare cases, when there is absolutely no choice and I feel I must do something instantly, I will use a physical correction. Most importantly, all corrections are effective only if they're *fast!* Speed dazzles dogs, while slow, late responses have the wrong effect. Knowing how and when to administer an effective physical correction takes a solid understanding of why your dog did what she did, split second timing and an ability to administer the lowest level correction necessary to get the point across. It seems that beginner's tendencies are to either make a correction which is too soft (and the dog thinks you're playing) or too hard (and the dog becomes defensively aggressive). So save physical corrections until you're sure you know when and how to do them, and for now, remember that you are always better off teaching a dog what *right* is, rather than what *wrong* is.

EXERCISES

Settle Down

Go out of your way to intentionally excite your dog (this way you have control over his responses, because you can stop being exciting any time). Then say "Settle" in that low, inhibiting voice you've practiced, and stop your arousing antics. Praise, throw a toy or give Fido a bit of liver immediately, and talk in low, long soothing tones to keep him quiet. Then try it again. Repeat this stimulating/settling exercise two or three times each, a couple of times each day. After several weeks of practice, ask your dog to settle when he really *is* excited, being sure to make him glad he listened to you. Start with mildly exciting situations and gradually over the next several months, ask your dog to "settle" during times of increasing excitement. You might also expect him to stay settled for longer and longer periods of time, but don't combine extra high excitement with especially long periods of being "settled." One step at a time!

Come

Starting today, make calling your dog a *game*, not a command. You are conditioning your dog to feel good when you call him to come, not expecting him to willingly leave that bratty squirrel he just found. Remember that these sessions should be short, upbeat, and scattered throughout the day. You must *not* say "No" or correct him in anyway, nor should you call "Come!" when you are sure your dog *won't* come ... unless you are willing to *patiently* go and get him. Whenever your dog doesn't come when called, go and get him (and his attention), and then encourage him to follow you. See the following section titled "Training Your Dog to Come on Command" for detailed instructions.

Sit, Lie Down, and Stand

In general, practice in short sessions, interspersed throughout your day, with a maximum of 4 to 5 sits each session. Try to end on a good response, even if it's not perfect. Be sure to practice this, as all signals, in different parts of your house, yard, or other safe outdoor areas. Stand squarely in front of your dog and use your smelly little tidbit to move your dog into the position you want. Remember to have the food right at the dog's nose, and then *lure* him into position with your combination lure and visual signal.

For "Sit," hold the food right at your dog's nose (not too high or he'll jump), and move your hand back toward his tail. Lots of dogs will follow the food with their nose and finally sit down as their nose goes up. If Ginger sits, immediately pop the treat into her mouth. If she just backs up, do this in a corner so that she can't. For now, don't even bother saying the word "sit." Dogs learn faster if first you work on the behavior and then associate the action with a verbal signal from you. Once she sits reliably to your food lure, (usually in the first or second session) say "sit" as she sits. After a few days of practice, begin to emphasize the upward sweep of your hand, rather than using it to lure their noses up and your dog will start to learn both the word and the visual signal.

For "Down," get him sitting first, then slowly move the food straight down to the ground, not too far forward. Start by sitting parallel to your dog and gently place your closest hand on his back, behind his shoulders. Slowly move the lure down toward the ground, moving the treat back to his nose if you lose his attention. Many dog will lie down to get the treat (this takes longer than getting them to sit, be patient). If Fido just won't lie down, *gently* push downward and slightly sideways with the hand on his back, but try to use the food to lure him down rather than forcing him into lying down with your other hand. The microsecond he lies down give him the treat. Practice two to five times a session.

For "Stand," simply wiggle the food in front of his nose and slowly sweep your hand straight forward to get him up from a sit or down. Be sure to say the signal *as he does it,* (not before or after), and to release the food the instant he has completed the action. Once he is reliable, begin to reward with food intermittently, not every time! It often takes a dog only a few days to respond reliably to a clear visual signal for "Sit" and "Stand," while "Down" may take some dogs much longer to learn without luring them with food or toys.

Finally, *observe* this week, and pay special attention to the way you move and speak when talking to your dog. Notice how your voice sounds and how your body is positioned. Does your voice make a statement or ask a question? Do you cock your head as you say "Sit?" If so, which signal is your dog learning? Pay attention to your dog's response— watch to see what he does immediately after you make a signal. Don't be too hard on yourself and think, "Boy, am I slow" or "I'm no good at training my dog!" This kind of thinking is not allowed! No, no...Bad Human! It will just make things worse. Simply observe like a scientist. You don't care what you do, you're just recording data! If you are inconsistent, say "Isn't that interesting. I said that two different ways within just two seconds. Hmm…" If you begin to notice these things, your mind will begin to fix them for you, but you must notice them first! Once you become aware of what you do, your brain will begin to tell your body to send out consistent signals. I guarantee that your dog will love her new, consistent and now-oh-so-understandable human. Whew! What a relief!

Training a Dog to Come on Command

Signals

Decide as a family what acoustic signal you will use to call your dog. Use it and *it alone* when you are serious about getting your dog to come to you. Varying how you say it, and using synonyms like "C'mon" and "C'mere" are a sure-fire way to confuse your dog. A good signal to use is your dog's name, said in a relatively flat tone, followed by the word "Come!" said in a rising, higher tone. I like to immediately follow this with hand claps, which are the most effective noises that I know of to motivate a dog to come to you. (They were also the most effective sounds in a laboratory study on five month old puppies.) If your dog has learned to ignore the word "Come," you might want to use "That'll Do," an old standby of Scottish shepherds. You could also use your dog's name said twice. In both cases, say the words with the second note higher in pitch.

Only use this command if you are willing to go and get your dog if he doesn't come. Otherwise he'll learn to ignore that silly noise you keep making. I think it's a good idea to have a casual signal, that means "Come over somewhere closer to me, sometime pretty soon." This will be far cry from your formal Come signal, which means: "Drop what you're doing this *instant* and run like Lassie toward me as though there's *nothing* you'd rather do!! Hand-claps, whistles, or high repeated notes like "pup pup pup pup!" are good acoustic signals for this casual message.

Remember also that dogs primarily communicate with visual signals. Dogs perceive a bow as a signal to approach for play, so bending over or squatting down is often a very effective way of *helping* your dog to approach. They also love to chase, which is why the games described below emphasize situations where your dog gets to run after you. These chase games teach your dog that coming is fun, and that's the key to establishing a reliable recall later on in life.

When and Where

- Play "come" games with your dog anytime during the day. Keep each session very short (how much do you learn when you are bored?). Be sure to play in *lots* of different environments and in short sessions scattered throughout the day.

- Begin in an area with no distractions. That means no other dogs, no neighbor children playing next door, no wafting odors of chicken broth floating in from the kitchen. For the first few weeks, do this when you are the *only* game in town. Around the third week or so, (depending on how well he is doing), begin to play these games during *low level* distractions like other people walking by a long way away, somewhat interesting, but not enthralling smells or mildly interesting noises. *Gradually*, over a period of months, work your way up to playing these games during higher level distractions. Calling your dog to come away from company at the door or while chasing a rabbit is the astrophysics of dog training; so start with first grade and work your way up to college.

The Games

The Chase Game. Start no more than five to ten feet away from your dog. Call his name, say "Come!" and start to clap, smooch and/or wave a stick around. As soon as he looks at you, immediately run away from your dog! The faster you run, the more encouraged he will be to follow you. As you run, continue clapping your hands encouraging him by running away and saying "Gooooood Dog!" Note how different this is from some methods, where the owner says "Come", and then forces the dog to approach them. It is much more effective to get the dog to approach you willingly and happily as though it were a game.

Once your dog has had the fun of a chase, squat down and open your arms to help direct him toward your body. If he runs past you, just get up and take off clapping and running the other way! Next time, anticipate his "zig" with a "zag"…just begin to run backward again in another direction when he's about 10 feet from you. You just turn the tables—play "hard to get" yourself before he has a chance to. When he arrives say "Good" and touch his muzzle on the side quickly and take off running the other way, or give a food reward or throw his ball. Food is a fine reward, but be sure to use it only as one of *many* rewards. Most dogs respond as though playing chase is the best reward of all, but be sure that the chase game is always one way—don't *ever* chase your dog back!

Your job here is to know exactly what will make your dog be glad he came. If he's not thrilled he came back to you, why should he do it next time when there's a cute little poodle across the street? Every dog is different: lots of dogs love to play chase, others want treats and ball play, while terrier-types can't resist that new squeaky toy you just bought that sounds ever so much like a mouse.

The Family Circle Game. Play this game with several people in a circle. Each person should say "Spot, Come!" and then clap, play bow and run away from the dog. Give a quick pet or food reward when he responds, then take your hands away from the dog and let another person call him. If your dog begins to simply run back and forth between people without waiting for a signal, give him credit for being smart, but be sure to reward him only if you say "Spot, Come!" Just ignore him if he runs to you on his own.

The Opportunity Knocks Game. Call "Spot, Come!" when you put his food bowl down, when he follows you as you walk toward the door, when he wakes up when hearing the leash jingle. Go ahead and call "Spot, Come!" when he's *already* coming to you! Why not? The idea is to teach an association between the sound and the action. Who cares *why* he came! The idea is to make his coming to you the most wonderful fun thing he can imagine, so do everything you can to teach him to associate the signal with something fun. Avoid calling "Come!" to do something that Spot truly hates, like trimming

11

his nails or putting him in his crate when he still wants to play.

Hide and Seek. This is my favorite game for older puppies, because I'm still fast enough to beat them, but just barely. We get totally lost in our game; I forget I'm training, and Spot learns to love those great noises that I make. First clap to get Spot's attention, then call "Spot, Come!" and take off in the other direction. Run and hide behind a tree, bush, building or chair. If you can really hide so that your dog has to find you, all the better! This seems to work just as well when the dog knows where you are, you know that the dog knows where you are, the dog knows that you know…etc, etc. I'll scrunch behind a tree that couldn't hide me if my life depended on it, squeal when the dog catches up and "finds" me, play tag around the tree awhile and then either take off for another "hide" or stop and giggle with my dog. After three or four chases, throw a toy, give a treat or make a fuss over how clever and quick he is, and then let him sniff around on his own for awhile.

An important caution here—chase games are great, but be sure your dog doesn't catch you literally—nipping at your pant legs or jacket should never ever be allowed. (This is a common problem if young children play this unattended with young dogs. Be sure you are there to insure that the game is about Come training, not "catch the kid!") If this happens while playing the chase game, try carrying a ball or stick and throwing it behind you before the dog gets to you (wave it as Spot runs toward you to redirect his attention onto it). Be sure that you are starting far enough away from the dog that he gets to run after you for awhile.

Lost Dog. An important variant on Hide and Seek is to take your dog somewhere new, where he is loose, but is not in any danger. Once he gets distracted by those new exciting smells, you quietly hide behind a tree or bush. Watch his face when he comes up for air and realizes he's lost you. If he looks absolutely panicked, squeak or smooch to get him looking in your direction, then duck your head and "let" him find you. If he starts looking seriously for you, let him work at it for awhile. If he puts his head down, lost in the joys of squirrel scent and seems oblivious to where you are, you probably want to skip this game. Some dogs just don't read the books. In any case, it's best to do this with young pups. The older a dog is and the less freedom he's had, the longer it will take for him to care where you are. It's one of the universal ironies of dogdom—the more freedom they have, the more they want to be with you.

On or Off Leash?

If at all possible, do all of the above games *off leash*. The more your dog is on a leash, the less inclined he will be to listen to you off leash. Make every effort to get the dog outside in a safe situation where you can do this without a leash. If you live where it's not safe to let your dog off leash outside, play the above games inside, and outside let the dog drag a long, light line (maybe 20 or 30 feet long). But try, if you can do it safely, to not hold onto the end of the line. If you're playing chase outside and your pup sees a squirrel across the street, you can usually grab the end of the line before he gets too far. This avoids panicked chases *toward* your dog, which only teaches him that he can beat you in a foot race. Once you have the line, wait until he is about at the end, and then say, "No" or "Hey" in a gruff voice—right before he gets to the end of the line. Don't jerk to whip your dog back through the air, unless your next door neighbor is a canine chiropractor. Just use the leash to stop your dog, then *let the line go slack*. Call "Spot, Come!" again, clap and run backwards, encouraging him to chase you back into the yard. Safety is always first, so if your dog might run into a road take no chances. In that case, make every effort to work on "Come" training outside somewhere that is safe: neighbors fenced yards, fenced play areas at training centers and boarding kennels, tennis courts, etc.

How Long Will This Take?

That's a tough question to answer, because so much depends on your dog. Two of my Border Collies have simply never not come when I called. The first day I had her, at one year of age, Lassie turned around in mid-air while tearing up a hill at 25 miles an hour and hit the ground running full tilt to me. No one ever trained her, or her father Luke for that matter, to come when called. She just does. (See why I call her Lassie?) Tulip, my independent Great Pyrenees is five years old now, and comes 99.9% of the time, but Tulip would never come away from a rabbit or deer until she was three years old. I'm just as proud of her as I am of the Border Collies, she just took much more work! Every dog is different. You can also expect your dog to change: reliable young pups can become rebellious teenagers before they settle back down again as adults.

Perhaps what's most important is to understand how important it is to gradually expect your dog to come through increasing levels of distractions and distances away from you. You will have the most luck if you set up situations where you have control, and teach your dog to come when called, no matter what the situation. This is very different than just waiting for something to happen, yelling "No" at King as he dashes off and then coping with the problem after the fact. Once you've done a month or two of the games above, keep playing the games and making come fun, but add "proofing" your dog through distractions as described below.

How to Compete with Distractions

Remember: teaching your dog to come to you in the house with nothing else to distract him is just step one in your training program. Calling him to come away from something *really exciting* like a yummy dead squirrel or kids playing soccer or that cute-little-Pomeranian-in-heat down the block is step 100. You simply can't go from step one to step 100 without helping your dog along the way, step by step. The steps in between are really different levels of distractions (or competition for your dog's attention) so create distractions yourself so that you can work on them in a *controlled* manner.

Use your common sense about what level of distraction to begin with: start with minor ones and slowly work up to more exciting situations. Do not, for example, start out right away calling your dog to come as he takes off after a rabbit! If he's coming well in the house, for example, take him outside when the neighborhood is quietest, and ask him to come when he's still quite close to you. Don't ask more than two or three times, or he'll get bored. Gradually work up to asking him to come if there are distractions around.

Gradually increase the difficulty of ONE of the following factors:

- Your *distance* from the dog

- The *intensity* of the distractions (start small and move up)

- The intensity of the *combined distractions* (i.e. are you asking him to come away from something moderately interesting, in a quiet room…or something interesting in a busy park with lots of things dividing his attention?)

Remote Corrections

Say you called your dog's name, said "Spot, Come!," clapped, and ran backward, but Spot kept sniffing the ground, ignoring you. If this happens, simply go closer to him and call again. If you get no response, then go all the way to the dog and get his attention with an abrupt "Hey" or "No." Then ask him to come again, as if nothing had happened, remembering to bow down in an inviting play bow. You can say the the "No" or the dog's name in a low, threatening tone, but the "Come!" part of the signal *must* be friendly. The key is to *always* get your dog when you call, no matter how long it takes. If it takes ten minutes for him to finally return to you, making you late for an important meeting, say "I hate you, you furry slime mold" in a sweet, happy voice while you smile through your gritted teeth.

If verbal corrections have no effect on your dog at all, try a "remote correction." Begin using remote corrections by putting something down that you know your dog will like, but can only sniff or investigate (like great food inside a container, for example). Go about five feet away and call Spot to come, being careful to say his name first, then call "Come!" in a rising, happy voice.

If he turns and looks at you, *immediately* say "Good Dog," bend forward in a play bow, keep clapping and saying "Good Dog" and continue to move backward. When your dog gets to you, make him *truly happy* he came—keep running, get all excited, give him food, throw a toy, etc. Then say "Ok" and let him go sniff the distraction again (and maybe get the treat inside).

If you get no response, this time throw something as you repeat "No!" The object should land noisily beside (not on!) your dog. Be sure it lands beside your dog, or on the other side of him from you. Don't throw it so that it blocks your dog's path back to you. As he looks up, call "Come!" again, clap and move backward, making Pooch more than glad he came by giving him a great treat, starting a chase game or letting him have access to what is in the container.

Repeat this a few times, looking for your dog to stop sniffing when you say "No," and come back to you without you having to throw anything. If she does, *jackpot!* Give Peaches *all* the treats in your hand so that she is mind-boggled about what she just did! This is where your knowledge of your dog as an individual is important—only you know what Peaches really wants. Be sure she gets it for such a difficult response or she'll ignore you next time.

Don't worry if your labrador happily picks up the empty pop can you just threw! What matters is that she stopped what she was doing when you said "No," which is the right response. If what she wants is the pop can as a reward, fine! Your dog doesn't need to be afraid of the object you throw, it just needs to be distracted. The best things to throw are empty pop cans with a few pennies inside (tape the top shut), bean bags, paper back books…use anything that makes a loud noise that your dog will startle to when he hears it land. Do be careful of sound sensitive dogs: some dogs are terrorized by pop cans (one Sheltie in training class was so scared he was afraid to come back in the room the next week, poor thing!). Use the lowest level noise you need to get a response out of your dog.

These "set ups" work wonderfully to convince your dog to come away from distractions. They teach your dog that you can be everywhere in some Zeus-like way, able to strike lightening no matter where you are. And you also get to be the good guy, since the scary thing landed over by the dog, but you're across the room, all sweetness and light. Sneaky, huh? Oh well, it works great, and may save your dog's life someday. Just be sure that your dog gets something wonderful for coming away from that bowl of liver or luscious dead squirrel (go ahead, let him roll in the squirrel this time!), and he'll start learning to come when you call, no matter what the distraction.

Using a Long Line

If the remote correction isn't working, set your dog up by putting him on a long, light lead. Let him drag it around for awhile, hopefully until he ignores it. Call him to come in the middle of an especially great sniffing session. If he doesn't come to your signal, grab the end of the lead and give him a light, quick snap as you say "No," followed *instantly* by an equally quick release. Use the line to get him looking toward you—then let it go slack. Run backward and encourage the *right* response as you did above. *Do not* just pull the dog in like a fish on a line! He must make his own decision about what he is going to do. I much prefer training without a leash at all, because the dog then is free to make his own decisions. Only use this method if you have no choice. With some dogs this works very well, especially while they are adolescents. The worst problem with line training is that most dogs learn when the line is on and when it is off, and behave accordingly. So always work *off leash* whenever you can, correcting your dog if necessary, and *rewarding* an approach toward you.

Stay Cool

Never, ever, ever express anger at your dog when he finally gets to your feet…even if you're furious! If you do, he'll be sorry he came and less likely to come when you call him the next time. It helps me a lot to think up nasty things to say to them, when they finally do come ("You look like a cat" is fun to say. What an insult! I'm also fond of: "I hate every hair on your body you furry slime mold."!) But again, keep your voice sweet and happy so Fido is glad he came or he'll learn to avoid you when you call come.

A Reliable Recall is Going to Take Time…

But it's worth it. Remember, the more freedom your dog has, the more he'll choose to stay with you. Accordingly, there is no other signal I know that is so valuable in having a healthy, happy dog. If your dog comes when you call, he can run free at the park, go on country walks, or run with a bunch of doggy buddies. So keep at it, and don't be discouraged if your dog regresses sometimes. Don't we all! Keep the faith, work hard, and have fun…and someday Spot will turn around in mid-air when you call, running to you like Lassie, and your heart will swell with joy and love, and it will all seem worth it.

Chapter 2

Learning Summary

POSITIVE REINFORCEMENT

Animals will learn to do anything fastest and most reliably if they are *positively reinforced* immediately upon doing it. Positive reinforcement is anything that makes your dog more likely to repeat what he was doing right before he got the reinforcement. Your challenge is to figure out what the best reinforcements are for your dog. They are not necessarily what make *you* feel good, or even what you might *think* your dog likes. Some dogs like food best, some like certain kinds of petting, some like running after you, and some like fetching a ball. Besides individual preferences, all individuals like different things at different times, so you will have the best results by *varying the reinforcements.* For example, no matter how much you love chocolate, or back rubs, or professional basketball, what if it was the *only* good thing you ever got for anything you ever did? Just exactly how many Hershey's kisses can any one person eat, anyway? (OK, OK, bad example.) Even if you're as much a chocolate lover as I am, do you really *always* want another chocolate kiss? Wouldn't you like, oh, a salary raise on occasion, or even just a glass of milk to go with your chocolate chip cookies? We tend not to generalize that to our dogs, and act as though saying "good dog" or a pet on the head is enough to get a dog to do anything, anytime, anywhere.

Using Treats

I often start with food (let your dog tell you what food she really wants, don't make assumptions), and *quickly* move on to other rewards. Most of the dogs that I have worked with can get a bit jaded about food treats or petting, especially if you give them out for free. You can avoid this by using food, but only giving it to her occasionally once she understands what the signal means. That way food is a surprise, not a *bribe.* As soon as your dog sits to your visual cue (usually after only a few days of practice with a food lure), reward her with a joyous hand clap and dash into another room! Or toss a ball or give a chest rub—if in fact your dog loves these things. My dogs love it when I play "hide and seek," take them on walks, give them steak, or rub their bellies…but the *ultimate*

17

reward for them is to herd sheep. That's why I train "Heel" on the way to the barn. If they forge ahead, I turn back to the house (sigh), but if they are good, we continue on to the barn. Keep in mind there is *no* leash involved here, and thus no physical correction. The *punishment* is simply not getting what they wanted. This is just one example of finding the right motivator for each signal—you must figure out for yourself what your dog likes best, and then insure that she only gets it by *earning* it. If you can't put a lamb in your pocket, then use tennis balls, Kong toys, sticks, chase games, belly rubs, or access to freedom to make your dog glad she did what you asked!

Most importantly, understand that your *dog* defines what *is* and what *is not* a reinforcement, not you! The most common mistake I see people make is to pet their dog on the head when she did something difficult, like coming away from a big distraction. The dog squints her eyes and backs away, and the owner never notices that the poor dog didn't want to be petted at all right then (especially not with those irritating pats on the top of her head! Ugh!) Think about it, do you *always* want a back rub? Even when you're giving a public talk? Trying to concentrate on something? None of us want *anything* at any given second, anytime, anywhere. Why should your dog be different?

Praise

Praise is a wonderful way to reinforce your dog, but don't assume your dog will jump through hoops the first time you say "Good Dog!" Big deal. Would two meaningless words like, "Woos Flam!" be enough to stop you from eating chocolate chip cookies and solve an algebra problem? "Good Girl" is meaningless to your dog (and therefore, ineffective) until you *condition* her to feel great when you say "Gooood." It's easy to do. Many of us do it without realizing it, but it works better if you do it consciously. Simply say "Good" while your dog eats, while you massage her, while her body wags from the shoulders back—whenever your dog is *internally* feeling good, say "Gooood." Eventually your dog will seek out the sound, because it has the power to help her *feel* good. I like to say "Gooood" in a relatively low, quiet voice to praise, but not over-stimulate my dogs.

Note that some dogs are highly motivated to get you happy and excited and will turn somersaults just to hear you say "Good Dog" in an excited voice. If you have a dog who lives to make you happy, count your blessings and appreciate each and every day with Lassie the wonder dog. However, most of us live with "normal" dogs, who have minds of their own (whose mind do we expect them to have anyway?). These are the dogs who need to be conditioned to love the sound of "Good Dog." Luckily, all dogs like to feel good, so teach Queenie to feel good when you say "good dog" and eventually she'll work to hear it.

Petting

All petting is not equal, so observe your dog carefully to see which type he likes best. Most dogs dislike pats on top of the head (some wolf handlers use head pats to get pushy, dominant wolves from getting in their face; I use two strong pats to tell my dogs to "go away" when I'm busy). You can pretty well be sure that Fido won't come again if you use head patting as a reinforcement. I'm amazed at the number of novice dog owners who slap their dogs on top the head, never noticing the dog backing away and grimacing. So watch your dog: he'll tell you what he likes if you pay attention.

TIMING

Dogs don't read minds, and they don't arrive pre-programmed to speak English. That is why timing is about 90% of good training. If a dog doesn't know what you want, the only way she can find out is by linking an act and a consequence together in time. If you want to reward her for urinating outside, don't watch her go, then wait until she returns and then give her a treat. What's the treat for? Returning to you, no doubt, because that's what she just did. Rather, give her the treat *the instant* she is done, so that she associates it with urinating, not trotting back to you.

A great way to practice good timing is during the "Come" exercise. You want to say "Come" the *instant* that your dog looks at you, and then switch to "Good Dog!" the *instant* that he moves toward you. Early in our training (you've noticed by now who's getting trained, right?) most of us humans say "Good Dog" after the dog has taken two to three strides. But that's a bit late. The hard part of a recall, from the dog's perspective, is re-directing their attention off what they were doing, and moving their attention and their body toward you. So you want to give them feedback the instant that they start that first lean in your direction. Great trainers say "Good Dog" as the dog's body moves toward them, just as the dog begins to take that first stride. Although a tasty treat or another chase game is a great idea after the dog actually gets to you, remember to time your "Good Dog" when the dog first starts doing the right thing, not after he's done.

Work on your timing with all your exercises: reinforcements should be given immediately as your dog initiates the right action. Corrections should occur the micro-second she does something wrong. This is part of the sport of dog training. You can learn it just as you learn any other sport, by practice, practice, practice, and good coaching. If you are lucky enough to have a video camera, have a friend tape you while you're training, and then play it back looking to see how your behavior synchronizes with your dog's. It's a great learning experience, whether you're a pet owner or interested in becoming a professional trainer.

Frequency and Duration of Training Sessions

Frequency and duration are vitally important aspects of your dog's learning. Many training books insist people train at the exact same time every day, only once a day, and only after the dog has been crated for an hour. For the life of me I don't understand why. Then you'd have a dog who listened to you once a day, just after he got out of his crate. Since life seems to happen to most of us all day long, I use the opposite approach. I ask my dogs to listen to me any time, surprising them with a quick surprise "sit" on the way to the door, asking for a short "Lie Down/Stay" on a walk, playing at "Stand" or "Come" as part of our daily routine. That's when I need my dogs to listen, so that's when I train. Keep your training sessions *very short,* and scatter them throughout the day. Avoid one long, boring training session. I have to fight for an extra half hour of training time any day of the week, but I *always* have 30 seconds to work on "Sit" or "Come!"

By integrating signals *throughout* your day, you can also make obedience relevant to the dog. (You want your dog to think "Oh, yeah. I get it! If I sit when she makes that silly noise, I get my dinner, my walk, my belly rubbed, my…! Boy, humans sure are *easy* to train! Let's see what else I can train my human to do.")

Some Things to Keep in Mind:

- Be thoughtful about *when* you train. Don't set up a nine month old pup to practice stay right after you've let her out of her crate; she simply can't sit still.

- Don't work on *too many different types of things* within one session. You can fry your dog's brain by expecting her to learn too many new things at once, just like you felt in school when you were overwhelmed with too much information.

- You also should *avoid training conflicting things* together. For example, don't hype your dog up with lots of exciting chase games and then expect a young pup to settle down mid-stream for some long down-stays. This is a great exercise at the intermediate level, but be careful of setting your dog up to fail in the beginning stages.

- *Help them be right at first, and they will learn to succeed.*

Schedules of Reinforcement

Schedules of reinforcement, or the consistency with which a dog is reinforced, is also very important in effective training. For example, what if a dog is highly motivated to do something that we don't appreciate? Say, for example, your dog is barking to get out of the crate. You give in because you're tired of listening to the noise, thinking just once won't hurt. *Just once* couldn't do *more* damage, because the dog learns that she won't be reinforced every time, but *if she just keeps it up,* she'll eventually get what she wants. Thus the dog that begs at the table because Aunt Polly snuck her treats last month is still waiting for that next goody. If you give in every third week, when you are too tired to hold out, she'll learn to beg for at least three weeks. That's why raising a pup with a large family can be such a challenge—it's hard enough to be consistent yourself.

There is good news here, however. The same principle that causes unwanted behavior to be easily reinforced by *just this once*, allows you to reward desired behavior erratically, too. Even little pups first learning "Sit" and "Lie Down" to the food lure should only get the food sporadically just as soon as they get the idea (two to three days?). I would go as far as saying you must *not* reward them every time at this point. If you do, they give up quickly if you don't have liver in your pocket. This is the biggest danger of using food in training. Unless you use food only occasionally, your dog will begin to check out whether you have those Snacker Snoozles. If you're empty handed, Misty will be long gone. This is easily prevented. Simply never let the dog expect to get food for a correct response, but let her know she *might* get it next time.

Think of it as your dog being a gambler and you the slot machine…maybe she'll get it, maybe she won't! But you *don't* want to be a human Coke machine, who is expected to *produce* when given fifty cents (or a paw in the lap!). Remember to *vary both the rewards and when you give them.* Then your dog will learn to associate *being obedient* with a generalized feeling of well-being…rather than some specific event that she may or may not want at the time.

HABITUATION

Habituation is the process by which your dog essentially learns to ignore you (or any other event in life). *If you repeat a signal over and over again, and do nothing else, then you are actively teaching your dog that the signal is just background noise,* and therefore should be ignored. For example, say you've asked your dog to sit and she ignores you. Most of us tend to continue repeating the signal, often louder and louder, apparently in hopes that amplitude itself will get the dog to sit. But unless you create a situation where the dog sits while you are saying the word, she will learn that "Sit" is just another meaningless noise, like the wind through the trees, and should be filtered out. Repeating signals on occasion during training is certainly not a crisis, and probably helpful for young dogs with short attention spans. Just be sure that you don't give up until the dog "Sits." But avoid needlessly repeating signals once a dog is trained to understand the signal—this will just teach her to wait for you to repeat yourself before she obeys. If she doesn't sit after you've said it twice, repeating it louder isn't going to get you anywhere, but it will teach her to ignore that noise you keep making while she's busy sniffing for rabbit poop. So if she doesn't sit, then switch to a visual signal, touch her rump, gently take her collar and lure her into a sit with a treat—whatever it takes to be sure that you don't give up once you've said a command. Great trainers, by the way, have learned the hard lesson of when *not* to say anything, since they know if they say "Come" they simply can't stop until the dog has completed the action. Sometimes silence is golden!

WHO'S WALKING WHO?

All dogs need to learn that leashes are not harnesses designed to haul their owners around like sleds, so *without question* you need to teach your dog general "leash manners." If your dog hauls you around like freight, who is the pack leader here? So, at the very least, you want to be able to walk your dog feeling like you're in control, rather than following a loose cannon down the street. You'll be very glad if you also teach your dog a proper "Heel." Luckily, those lessons are closely related.

First off, let's start by keeping your arm attached to your shoulder. Remember that slow, continuous *pulling* elicits slow, continuous *pulling back!* If your dog pulls you a little, and then you pull a little back, and then he pulls a little harder…you are well on your way to training a professional sled dog. Mammalian muscles work on a principle of resistance, so if you pull just a little bit, your dog will be stimulated to pull back just a little bit harder. This cycle continues until taking the dog on a walk is more like punishment. One of my clients actually had his arm pulled out of his shoulder socket by a St. Bernard! And you thought *your* dog pulled.

First, ask yourself "Where is my dog's *attention?*" Whether on a perfect heel or just being polite on a leash, a trained dog always has part of his attention on you. Dogs who throw themselves forward in greyhound-like lunges are basically signaling that their owners have just become irrelevant. So you're first job is to teach your dog that it *pays* to pay attention to who's on the other end of the leash. You do that by being sufficiently interesting to make your dog glad they noticed:

FOLLOW THE OWNER GAME

Getting the Follow Game Started. The "follow the owner" game is simple, fun and critical for dogs at any age. Begin by deciding what you will use to reinforce your dog for his attention. Start with a lure that will *really* motivate your dog—food, squeaky toys, tennis balls, etc. Go somewhere quiet with few distractions, then put on your dog's leash. Just let the leash drag right now, don't worry about holding on to it. Now call your dog to you, then slap your left leg a few times with your left hand to focus your dog's attention in that area. As you do, *quickly* walk away from him while you wave your lure by your left leg. If the dog catches up to you, immediately give him reason to be glad he's beside you on your left side—give him a treat, a thrown ball, gooey praise, whatever works! Just be sure to do it the instant he's beside your left leg, not as he begins to move away. If he *ignored* you, either call his name or say "Ah!," clap your hands, do whatever necessary to get his attention, and then reward him for giving you his attention.

Now walk—or better yet trot, scamper, dash, or *run* in a different direction, just a few steps, and reward his attention again. Your goal is to move around in space such that he follows you, staying on your left side and getting lots of wonderful rewards for paying attention to you. Do this approximately 5 to 10 times for the first session, moving as quickly as possible. There are at least three goals here: to make your dog *glad* he paid attention to you, to teach him it's extra fun being by your left leg, and to teach your dog that you are a fascinating but totally *unpredictable* creature, who never goes in a straight line (boring), but turns and twists with no warning whatsoever. (With apologies to half the population, I call this my "crazy woman" routine.)

Should I say "Heel"? I wouldn't suggest that you use a verbal signal yet. Since the dog is just getting interested in the game, avoid "putting it on cue" until he knows what "it" is! Use the word "Heel" only after a week or so of this game, once it is going well for both you and your dog. After a few sessions with your dog dragging the leash, try picking the leash up in your left hand, if the dog is on your left, teasing the dog with the lure in your right hand (held around the front of your body and over to the left side) and stride away. Some people do better with the lure in their left hand and the leash in their right. Do what's best for you, just guard against holding the lure too far in front of you so that your dog is forced to get ahead of you all the time to follow it.

Loose Leashes! Your goal here is to keep the *leash loose.* If your dog gets in front of you and begins to gradually pull harder and harder, and *you* react by pulling harder and harder back, you have now entered the world of harnesses, draft horses, and sled dogs, and may enter a rope pulling contest…without passing Go or collecting $200! If, on the other hand, you respond by simply reversing yourself and going in the other direction, your dog is now *behind* you, wondering what happened. You can help your dog when you turn by slapping your leg (be sure not to shake the leash in his face) and bending your knees a bit, then be sure to reward him when he has caught up and is walking beside your left leg again. Most importantly, train yourself to turn a lot, speed up, slow down, alternately treat your dog with food or a toy and lots and lots of verbal praise when he is in the right position.

Short Sessions. Gradually increase the length of time you expect your dog to attend to you and the amount of external distractions. Like all your training, you are better off doing several short sessions every day rather than one long one. Ideally, do three or four short leash sessions each day, but don't be disheartened if you can't manage that. Once you begin training consistently, you'll be amazed at how fast your dog progresses. On the other hand, don't expect a 6 month old Golden Retriever to walk quietly on a leash through a flock of Mallard ducks for a half an hour. That's actually not too far from what a lot of people expect of their dog—leash walking a young dog around a neighborhood *rich* with new smells and noises, flirty little Lhaso Apso's and handsome German shepherds—all before they ever taught him to be polite on a leash in the first place! You are better off exercising your dog in your yard and other safe areas rather than inadvertently teaching him to pull you around the block.

To summarize, leash manners basically equate to a dog that doesn't pull on a leash. This can be taught by teaching a dog to "follow" you with the leash on by rewarding him for paying attention to you while staying on your left side. Anytime he goes too far ahead of you, simply reverse and walk the other way, rewarding him when he gets back to your left side. Practice this now, and stay tuned for more leash exercises in the next chapter.

EXERCISES

Off

"Off" is such a handy signal to have, I use it every day. Basically it means "back up." Use it to get your dogs to back away from the door, to stop a forward lunge for the pork chop you just dropped or if Fido is about to sniff dog-hating Aunt Polly in some embarrassing place. You could use "No" also to stop your dog in these contexts, but I like Off best because it tells your dog what it is you want them to do.

Try the following to teach your dog the concept of "Off:" Put a small tasty food treat between your thumb and fingers. Sit down beside your dog so your hand can easily be at nose level. Say "Off" first, then move your hand right to your dog's nose (not above it). Be sure to say Off *before* the food arrives at the dog's nose. Hold the food a half inch away from the dog, and if she reaches for the food, don't pull back your hand or repeat "Off." Instead, tap her nose with a quick forward jabbing motion. (Be sure not to set your dog up to fail by holding the food above her nose, because then she'll try to reach for it by jumping up.)

Your behavior is entirely driven by your dog's: if Ginger reaches toward the food you tap her nose with your fingers. However, if she backs up just a bit, you say "OK!" and give her the treat. She should get the food as soon as she stops putting "pressure" toward the it (you'll learn to feel it as much as see it). When she does, say "OK," and let her move toward you for the food. *Do not move the food toward the dog*—you are trying to teach the concept of *forward* and *back*, and you want the *dog* to do that, not you!

This is really just Phase 1 of "Off" training. We'll talk about how to expand it in the next chapter. For now, work on this phase until your dog will not touch the food after you say "OK" without you having to tap her. Do *not* use this signal functionally yet—the dog isn't ready. (For example, don't wait for visitors and then say "Off" when the dog is all excited.) Only use Off during training sessions right now with the food in your hand. In the next chapter we'll generalize it for all-around use.

Heel

For a week or two just work on the "following" game, remembering to:

- Keep sessions very short at first and without distractions. Do the first sessions in a safe place without a leash by using smelly treats to get his attention.

- Vary your direction and pace *a lot*—being unpredictable is one of the keys to this working well.

- Keep the leash completely *loose* unless you turn away from the dog. Try not to use the leash to move the dog around in space, only to inhibit him from taking off. Use your voice, leg slaps, smooches, food treats or toys to convince your dog to move the right way, but don't *pull if you can help it!*

- Don't ever give a jerk correction for lagging behind—that will just make the lagging worse. Encourage your dog with interesting noises, by speeding up, or by using food…then *praise and treat* him when he has caught up.

- Give lots of verbal praise and treats for even a few steps of a good follow. Most people don't reward their dogs often enough when first teaching heel. Lots of toys, treats, and praise should be given when he is in the *right* position.

- Avoid long neighborhood walks while you're working on this. If that's not possible, then start your walk off with "follow" for just a minute, then let your dog have some freedom to sniff. Remember this works best in very short sessions—how long could you listen to a lecture about algebra while browsing in a shopping mall?

Come

Keep playing the Come game, always in short, fun sessions, and remember to NOT call "Come" if Misty is wallowing in cow pies (or otherwise totally distracted). It won't work yet! Go get her if you have to, but do not call "Come" repeatedly and then give up. Then Misty will learn to ignore you, because she will *habituate* to it as a noise rather than a signal. Keep this as a fun game, and be sure to play in lots of different contexts, in short, playful sessions, scattered throughout the day. Remember too, that coming in the kitchen is not the same as coming in the yard, so practice everywhere it is safe, preferably when your dog is *most likely* to pay attention to you.

Sit, Lie Down, and Stand

Begin using the food lure *less* and the visual signal *more*. "Sit" just to a hand signal is learned very quickly by most dogs, whereas "Lie Down" usually needs a longer duration of visual signals and food lures (patting the ground often helps). You might be ready to try one "Lie Down" with food in your signal hand and the second one with food in your other hand. Lure the dog down with the empty hand (which probably still smells like food), then reward with the other hand. Your dog will start learning that the reward comes, whether she notices food in the signal hand or not.

A caution about patterns: make sure you are not asking your dog to always "Sit, Lie Down and Stand" in the *same* order. If you do, he will learn a pattern, rather than each individual signal. It may be cute when they run through their entire repertoire in front of company, when you just gave one command, but it's not going to teach them what each signal really means, and will result in confusion (and usually mad owners) eventually.

Chapter 3

Whose House Is This, Anyway?

I know you love your dog. But if you love your dog you will do him no favors by catering to him, continually cooing over him or providing him with no boundaries. Dogs need to feel secure to be truly happy; and that means they need to feel secure that *you* will be the leader, and that they can count on you to take charge. But being the "leader" or being "dominant" is often misunderstood. It does not necessarily mean that you physically dominate your dog at every second. Rather, leadership is more of a mental quality, occasionally reinforced physically if necessary, but more often expressed by you providing confident direction. It *is* your house, after all—and you deserve the rights that go with the responsibility. Keep it that way, and your dog will love you better for it.

It's lonely at the top, so give your dogs a break and take over.
They'll love you for it, and that is what you want, isn't it?

The following suggestions are an effective and humane way to let any dog know that he or she is loved and cherished, safe and secure but *not* the leader of the pack. Keep in mind that love is not related to social status, and that most dogs live in relaxed harmony when the social hierarchy is clear, no matter where they stand in it. Dogs behave as though they prefer knowing that you are in charge, and often seem much happier when they understand that you have (finally!) taken charge. Following the advice below is much harder on you than on your dog, so be good to yourself in lots of ways while you're following this program!

The suggestions below are not practices that you must follow every second of every day, no matter how your dog behaves. There are plenty of times I pet one of my dogs when he or she comes up just to say hello. Who wants a dog if you can't ever pet it just for fun?! But you simply can't cater to your dog like a geisha girl either. Your dog is the one who drives your decisions about how to behave: Some dogs will take a mile if you give them an inch, some dogs can be downright spoiled and still come whenever they're called. All dogs can get into trouble eventually if they think they are in charge, so no matter how great your dog is, always be careful about catering to him and indirectly forcing him into the lead. It's lonely at the top, so give your dog a break and take over. They'll love your for it, and that's what you want, isn't it?

Petting

I think we pet our dogs for at least two reasons: it feels *really good* to us (and is indeed good for us; it lowers our blood pressure and heart rate), and it's a way to tell our dogs how much we love them. You'd think this would all work well, because so many dogs seem to love being petted as much as we love to pet them. The problem is that petting is *grooming* to dogs, as it is to most social mammals, and grooming is usually done *by subordinates to and for dominants*. When a dog comes up to you, pushes into your space and insists in some way that you pet him, he's not being sweet, loving or cute. He's *demanding* that you pet him. If you respond, you are submitting to your dog, and have just agreed to elect him pack leader. After all, if your dog can come up and say the equivalent of "*YO! Human! Pet me...Right now!,*" why should he let you take away the pork chop he just stole from the counter?

On the other hand, you can use your dog's desire for attention to motivate her to do what you ask. If she wants to be petted and you'd like to pet her, simply ask her to Sit or Lie Down first. Now she is learning that by being obedient and subordinate she can still get what she wants. Good Dog!

If you have had any trouble with any type of aggression with your dog, follow the ideas below to the letter. (And why wait for trouble? Most of us would have happier dogs if we kept the following in mind.) As your dog improves you can modify the instructions a bit, and allow yourself some free pets (for your sake more than for your dog!).

- Pet only for obedience (Come, Sit, Lie Down, etc.)

- Keep petting brief—Don't cuddle on the couch eating popcorn, mindlessly petting your dog while you watch a movie. When you stop what happens? She nudges you with her nose, and you, good little subordinate that you are, start petting again, right?

- If you want to initiate petting, call your dog to you, don't go to him.

If the Dog Demands Petting, Either:
- **Body Block** (see below) with your shoulder or elbow, leaning forward with your torso if the dog pushes into your space and then *look away* (fold arms, turn head up and away from the dog)

- and/or, ask for a Sit or a Lie Down, then pet.

Body Blocks

Owners who can only control their dogs with leashes have dogs who respect leashes, not owners. A leash can be a useful safety net and occasional training tool, or it can sabotage all your efforts to have your dog listen to you. If you always use your leash to control the movement of your dog, who is in control? Must be the leash. Congratulations, you've just elected a thin strip of nylon as the President of your house.

Dogs get and maintain dominance over each other in a number of ways. One of the most effective techniques is by controlling the use of *space* by other individuals, rather than by controlling every move the other dog makes. Dogs "herd" each other by simply imposing their body in the direction of travel of other dogs, and so can you. All you need to do is to insert your body in the dog's direction of movement and lean forward slightly. This, for example, is the best way to stop a dog from breaking a Stay: simply watch them like a hawk, *and as they start to get up,* lean your body toward them and raise your arms up and out to effectively block that space. Dogs are very sensitive to this visual signal, so lean backwards a bit when they settle back down or you will be putting too much "pressure" on them.

Use the same action to block other unwanted moves on their part. For example, what if your dog jumps up on you while you're sitting on the couch? You won't get control (or leadership) by pushing your dog away from you with your hands. I suspect that dogs think hands are simply our pathetic attempt to make up for not having muzzles, and respond by getting mouthy themselves. If you get firmer, they either think you *really* want to play or they become defensively aggressive. I have had great luck with what ethologists call "shoulder slams," where you pull your hands in toward your chest, and push the dog away with your shoulder, or elbow. Using your torso appears to be understood by dogs as a status related gesture, and is much more effective at stopping dogs from being physically pushy than using your hands. Notice that again you are leaning your body forward *into* the dog, effectively "taking the space" away from him.

Accordingly, don't let your dog stand in front of you and cause you to redirect your path. That's big time dominance in a canid society. If you're walking from point A to point B, and your dog stands in your path, just keep walking forward in tiny steps. Keep your feet on the ground and shuffle right through Fido (don't raise your feet up as if you were kicking him!). Let your dog pay attention to you and where you're going, not vice versa.

Learning to imagine an inviolate column of air in front of and around your body might be the one most important things you can do to let your dog know who's in charge. Spend a few weeks paying attention to which way your body is leaning when you work with your dog. For example, when he's jumping out of control when it's walk time: do you shift your weight back ever so slightly as the King leaps up at you (pretty understandable after all, since King weighs as much as you do!), or do you lean forward slightly to "take the space?" This can occur in units of microseconds and millimeters, but start out by exaggerating your actions until they become second nature. *(Caution: if your dog has bitten or seriously threatened you, please don't do this without getting professional help from someone who specializes in treating aggression.)*

Practice "Look Aways"

Don't let your dog demand anything (usually play or petting). If your dog gets "pushy," simply cross your arms, turn your head upward and to the side away from your dog. If the dog counters by moving to your other side (where your head is directed) turn your head away again.

If your dog is very dominant, this is a good thing to do often when your dog approaches you. Look away *consistently* if your dog has been very aggressive toward you—as a matter of fact, you should completely ignore him for several days if he has lunged, snapped or bitten lately.

Looking away is the visual signal sometimes given by dominant dogs toward subordinates and is very very different than the hard, direct stare that some books tell you to give your dog. Be careful of assertive stares—as best we know, they are invitations to fight rather than the actions of a well-established, confident but benevolent alpha (that's you!).

Lie Down and Stay

Teach your dog a good solid Lie Down and Stay. Start with one second stays for the first two days, then quickly work up to longer and longer ones (avoid distractions at this point). After three weeks, most dogs (except energetic juveniles) can handle a half-hour down stay during a quiet time of day when all the rest of the house is quiet. It works best for me to have them lie down between me and the television; that way we've both found a place to park and the dog is automatically in my line of sight!

Remember that your dog has to learn to stay through all kinds of distractions, and most novice dog trainers expect dogs to stay through difficult distractions much too early in training. So ask for long Down/Stays during quiet times, understanding that your dog will probably get up automatically if you do (so help them by visually signalling Stay before you move). Correct breaks with *Body Blocks*, not by simply repeating sit, down and stay over and over again. Pantomime your dog back into place, all the time remaining quiet and calm. If your dog gets up 25 times, then correct him or her 25 times with the same actions and tone of voice—do not include anger in your correction. Be very matter-of-fact. Most dogs do best if you work on this silently, except for a quiet "Stay" signal, always given in conjunction with a clear hand signal to help the dog know what you mean.

Wait at the Door

Alpha dogs have "priority access to limited resources," which means that they get to push out the doorway first to get to something they want. That is why so many dog fights occur at doorways over who gets to go out first. This is not different than our species—would you barge into the Pope to get out the door first? If your dog runs into you to get to something she wants, she's not exactly being respectful of you. And respect is what it's all about.

You can handle the rush to the door in two ways: one is to say "sit" and "stay," going through the door first and then releasing the dog to follow you. I think a much better way is to use *Body Blocks* to herd the dog away from the door, then block her again if she tries to go through first without you saying OK. Avoid using the leash—that is simply an admission to the dog that you have no control. Control the space in front of the dog and you control the dog.

Say you're going out on a walk with your dog. Ginger will probably get to the door first, since dogs all seem to move at the speed of light if they want something. You can't control her if you're behind her, so simply slide your body in between your dog and the door and "herd" her backwards about three or four feet from the door. She'll probably continue to try to get around you to the door, but keep blocking her with your legs (by moving sideways and *forward*) until she pauses. Then move to the door (still facing her) and partially open it. (Have your dog on leash if necessary for safety's sake, but do *not* use the leash to control her. Have someone else hold a leash if possible, or tie it to a railing, but don't use the leash to block her; let your body do it.) Most dogs move forward as they see the door open—this is when you should step forward, blocking that space, and again herd your dog away from the door. Once she backs up, you step aside from the open door and give her a chance to make her own decision. Always give your dog a choice—don't continually block the opening by draping your body over it—rather step back a bit so that the dog makes her own choice about whether to wait or to barge through. At the first sign of hesitation, you step through and say "OK." No need to treat here: what she wanted was out the door, and now she knows how to earn it.

Four on the Floor

Dogs interpret an increase in vertical height as an increase in status. Period. End of sentence. It's a *symbol* to us, but a synonym to them. I've seen sweet a puppy-loving female dog turn into a furry chain saw when the owner inadvertently picked a puppy up and held it above the adult female's head. Apparently it looked like the puppy was challenging her for status, and since the pup was seven weeks old and she had seven years under her belt, she was not impressed. Although there's no good research on this, my clinical work suggests that dogs who sleep up on the bed are especially impressed with themselves. After all, they are up high and allowed in the royal sleeping quarters. They *must* be important, look where they get to sleep!

31

The solution is simple, although I know it's hard on some owners who love to cuddle with their dog. Keep dominant dogs on the floor—not up on chairs, couches or beds (especially if you are in the room). If you want to cuddle, *you* get down on the floor, ask for some obedience and then pet.

This seems impossible to owners whose dogs have slept on the bed for years, but in my experience dogs adapt to this change in routine amazingly fast. An easy way to accomplish this is to leash to dog to the leg of the bed while you sleep. Just take them there each night, pet the ground (you can make them a bed if you think they'd like it) and say "Go to Bed." You might give them a toy stuffed with food to sweeten the pot. Be sure you never go to a dog who has shown status-related aggression in the past and try to pull it off the bed or couch by his collar. This is too dangerous. Rather, call the dog to come off, using positive reinforcement to insure he'll be glad he came.

Teach "Off"

Pack leaders can warn an individual off of some resource with a quiet growl and a warning glance. Teaching your dog to back away from something (dropped food, a toy, your Aunt Polly who hates dogs…you get the idea!) is a wonderful way to impress your dog with your ability to "take charge." "Off" is especially valuable because it is so much like a "display" signal that high status wolves give to each other. You're not fighting, you're not being aggressive, you're simply calmly making the point that you get to say who gets the dropped pork chop on the kitchen floor!

If you did the exercises in the last chapter, then you've already started teaching your dog "Off" when you're holding a treat in your hand. Just to review, remember to move the treat all the way to your dog's nose as you say "Off," give her a chance to be right, but be ready to "bop" her nose gently if she tries for the food. As soon as she backs away, even if it's just a lean away from the treat, say "OK" and let her move forward to get the treat.

Food in the hand is different than food on the floor, so you must teach your dog to move back in each context when you say "Off" as a separate phase of training. While standing, ask your dog to sit or stand to one side of you. Say "Off" in a low voice, and then drop the treat on the other side so that you can move forward to block the dog from the treat if you need to. Be ready to Body Block her repeatedly until she stops trying for it and pauses. Immediately say OK, and let her have the food. Do *not* do this if your dog has been seriously aggressive over food, unless you are working one-on-one with a professional.

Gradually move farther and farther away from the food until you can say "Off" from across the room and have the dog wait to nose the toy or eat the food. Oh, the power!

Integrate Obedience into Your Day

I do not recommend having one or two "training sessions" each day. Rather, you should integrate obedience into your dog's day, such that it becomes part of life to them. Simply ask the dog to perform some action whenever it wants something (you to open the door, to play ball, to get dinner, etc.). Teaching Sit, Down and Stay can easily be accomplished by asking for one or two of those actions as you are playing, walking across the room, going outside, watching TV, etc. The key is to understand that dogs will work to get something that they want—your job is to know what your dog wants at that particular moment in time. No dog wants food all the time, and no dog wants praise all the time. Just like us, what they want varies from minute to minute. So use this principle so that it works for you rather than against you. Make obedience seem relevant to life so that your dog begins to learn: "Oh, I see, the way to control my environment and get what I want is to do what she says."

Leaders are in the Lead

Insuring that your dog will heel on cue is an important part of being "alpha." *After all, if your dog is in the lead, he's the leader, right?* "Heel" is the perfect way to teach your dog to pay attention to you, and to let you initiate where to go and how fast you get there. Remember, though, you can't teach a good heel simply by forcing your dog to stay beside you. Rather, follow the instructions from books or classes that emphasize positive reinforcement on how to teach heel as a *fun game* that you and your dog get to play together. Once they know what *right* is, you can use your authority to enforce it. Remember that dog packs don't have anything equivalent to "Heel" (or, from a dog's perspective, "walk slowly at a boring pace by your owner's left leg, ignoring all interesting things"), so it is up to us to teach our friends what we are talking about.

If you have a dog whose main exercise is a neighborhood leash walk, you probably don't want to keep Fido on "Heel" the entire time. I wouldn't either. The problem is easily solved…only let your dogs direct their (and therefore your) activity part of the time. Always begin and end with the dog responding to you rather than vice versa. The first few minutes when you leave the house is the perfect time to insist that your dog attends to you—after a few minutes (seconds at first) of a good job heeling, let him sniff to his heart's content. Since that's really what he wanted, it's the perfect reward! So ask for attention, and deference to you, as you leave and before you enter back into the house, and let your dog have the freedom he earned in between.

This is the time to add body blocks to your repertoire. When your dog is behind or beside you, turn left abruptly in front of and around him. Turn a full half circle so that you are now going the other way. If your dog's head was beside or behind you, your action will simply block his forward passage and cause him to pause a bit, look up at you as you move around in a circle, and tend to stay closer to your side. Give him a treat the micro-second you straighten out, assuming he is still in the right position. If you do this when your dog is the slightest bit ahead of you, you'll just run into your dog's ribs, he'll spurt out in front of you and you'll be wondering why I ever got you into this. So start when Fido is well behind or beside you. (It helps with exuberant dogs to first turn to the right, away from your dog. Now he's behind you and has to catch up. Before he does, turn left in a half circle around him.)

This blocking turn (really another Body Block) is the key to quickly teaching a dynamite heel. If your dog runs into your leg, because you did an abrupt turn in front of him, you have taught him that you control the space into front of him. He'll learn that you are absurdly unpredictable, so he'd better pay attention to you all the time because *you just never know what that crazy human is going to do next!* Now your dog is hesitating a little bit, beginning to look up at you, thinking about what you might be about to do, interested, walking by your left side—good grief, this looks like a *perfect* "Heel"!

Play

Dogs settle many of their hierarchy issues in play, so you need to be aware of how your play can either promote your dog up the ranks or keep him happily subordinate to you. Remember that *Alpha,* or the pack leader, *initiates behavioral change,* so anytime your dog demands something ("Play with me, *now!,*" "Pet me, *now,*" "Let me out *right now!*") he is electing himself pack leader. *You* should initiate play sessions, and *you* should be able to stop them with a quiet word.

Don't let your dog push you with his nose and demand petting. It's not sweet, loving, or cute... it's pushy.

Also, be very careful of tug of war games. Pack leaders get the "prize," and if you play lots of strength games with your dog and he always "wins" (i.e., you walk away when you're done and he still has the tug toy), then he's also just won dominance over you. Some people suggest never playing tug of war, and I wouldn't advise it if you've ever had any problems with aggression with your dog. If you haven't, and you really want to play tug, then be sure to take the toy and put it away when you're done. It's *your* toy, Alpha, remember?

Finally, don't ever "rough and tumble" wrestle play with your dog. I always feel like a witch when I say that, because usually some kind-hearted, dog-loving man's face falls when I do. Make no mistake about it: with some exceptions, this is a guy thing. Male primates engage in "rough and tumble play" so conspicuously that field researchers sometimes use it as an indicator of gender. Indeed, 95% of the people I see in my office who wrestle play with their dogs are men. So I always feel guilty taking away their fun, because there's no doubt that both humans and dogs love it. But, male or female, it teaches dogs to play rough with humans, and it *oh so very often leads to trouble.* Perhaps not with the person who started it, but more likely with the little girl whose parent's are suing you over the "play bite" to their daughter's face. Or to the younger, smaller family member who finds the dog constantly mouthing them and biting at their arm on leash walks. Instead, play ball, play frisbee, play soccer, let your dog chase you (not vice versa), teach heel like a game, teach "find it," train tracking, do tricks together, herd sheep, go hunting, have a wonderful joyful time together, but please, *please* don't wrestle with your dog.

A Review about Food

There is no reason not to use food to initiate a new command with your dog. The problem some people have is that they *always* give the dog food for compliance—and soon have a dog who *only* performs if you have food. You can easily prevent this, by simply using food intermittently and focusing on using other reinforcements to insure your dog is glad to be obedient. Use intermittent reinforcement in two ways: vary what the dog gets for obeying (food, praise, play, get to pee!, belly rubs, etc.) and don't always give the dog something—sometimes they should just do it! How many quarters would you put in a slot machine before you got something back? Now compare that to how many you'd put into a Coke machine if you didn't get your pop. If you always expect a reward, your behavior ceases quickly if you don't get something every time; but if you never know when the pay off will come you persist, just like you want your dog to do!

Alpha Roll-Over...Don't Do It!!!

Be careful about doing the often-advised "alpha roll-over" in which owners are told to flip their dogs over onto their backs and stand over them, growling and staring. This is supposed to be a good way to exert your dominance, because it is similar to behavior seen in a wolf pack. Well, yeah, you do see individuals exposing their bellies in a dominant/subordinate context in a wolf pack, but you don't see the alpha grab the subordinate by the scruff of his neck and flip him over onto his back except in an all-out fight. People don't win dog fights, so don't start one. In "passive submission" the lower status animal rolls over *voluntarily*—he isn't forced into it.

Leadership in canid packs is maintained by simple, subtle things: a directed gaze, a step forward or backward, the knowledge of who initiates and who responds. By the time you're at the "throwing onto backs stage," the hierarchy has broken down. It's not being maintained...it's in chaos. Starting a dog fight is the last thing owners who are not sure where they and their dog stand should be doing. It'll either scare your dog and elicit defensive aggression, infuriate a dog who thinks he's alpha and get you bitten, or communicate to Prince that you want to play roughhouse today (Oh Boy!!). Individual wolves and dogs are physically disciplined by high status individuals with "muzzle pins," in which the dominant grabs the subordinates muzzle and gives a corrective pinch. However, *nothing* is going to get me to advise owners to bite their own dogs on their collective muzzles! Keep in mind that you are often the role model for your dog: if you teach him that *you* get what you want by using force, then he'll be more likely to use it when he can get away with it. I have always argued that "force is the absence of real power." After all, if you really are powerful, why would you need to resort to physical force? You are much better off telling your dog to lie down and stay for an hour after disobedience than you are starting a dog fight.

EXERCISES

Off...Phase II

After your dog is completely reliable with the food in your hand (and will back away just at the sound of your voice), practice "Off" with the food somewhere else. Keep in mind that possession is the law in canine society, so once you no longer have the food in your hand your dog will work much harder to get to it first.

Start with two or three reviews of Off with the food in your hand. Now stand up, lure your dog to one side of you, say "Off" and drop the treat on the other side. Be sure to start with plenty of room between you and the dog so that you have time to block her when she goes for the food. Block your dog from getting the treat with a Body Block (remembering not to repeat "Off")—but be ready to block her *fast!* As soon as she withdraws and pauses, say "OK" and let her come and get the food. Remember to let your dog make her own mind up—give her the freedom to be right or wrong, and to learn from it.

Once the dog is 95% reliable on this with you close by, start practicing when you are a little farther away from the food. Substitute toys, sticks or anything else you think your dog might want. Over a few months you can expect your dog to back away from something that fell off the counter even if you are twenty feet away.

Wait

Unlike "Stay," "Wait" simply means pause for a moment. Use this signal mostly at doorways, in and out of your car and your house. It is very easy to teach, and glory be, takes very little practice.

Do the early training at home. Start with your body between the dog and the door. You're going to block the dog from going through the door with your body, and you can't do that if Missy is already in front of you. If your dog lunges to the door and presses her nose against it whilst dancing a jig, simply walk between her and the door, keeping your feet on the ground and shuffling your body toward the dog and away from the door. If Missy tries to go around you to the left, stop her with your lightening fast reflexes by moving to the left and blocking her path. Stay silent, and let your body do the talking at this point.

Once she's about four feet from the door, say "Wait" in a low quiet voice. As you open the door, be ready to block her with your body if she tries to bolt through. Once she looks as though she won't try again, say "OK" and let her trot out. Remember to let your dog make her own mind up—give her the freedom to be right or wrong, and to learn from it. Resist the urge to drape your body over the door like a curtain. Stand to the side so that she can chose what to do herself. Block her if she tries to go through, and say OK if she "waits" for you, Most dogs catch on easily by the end of a few days. Go out of your way to insure that *all* members of the family consistently have the dog wait at the door, rather than letting her barge through it. Be sure to remember to say "OK" if you use "Wait." They can also give *no signal*, and simply use your body to block the dog from going out the door first. Either way, *do not* use the leash to restrain your dog. Block him with your body, but don't restrain him with the leash.

Stay

Start with Micro-Stays! Your first Stay sessions should be *very short* for all beginning dogs—one second is plenty. Start with the dog sitting about two feet in front of you in a quiet room. Ask for a brief stay by saying "Stay" in a low quiet voice, and visually holding your palm toward her face. This is a great time to practice using your voice and your body in ways to help rather than hinder your dog. Saying "Stay?" with your voice rising will stimulate your dog to get up, not to stay still. You don't need to growl it out, just tell your dog to "Stay" in a quiet, low voiced statement. Think too about your visual signals: are you using the same one all families members use? Are you confusing her by moving your hand in a "sit" signal? Remember that she is desperately watching you, trying to figure out what you're saying, so help her by being thoughtful and consistent with your signals. (Speaking of confusing, don't hold food in your hand, or you will lure her forward.)

Be sure to say "Stay" only once. Back up a half step, holding your breath and looking directly at your dog. Don't move at first. After a *brief* pause, return to your dog and give her a treat. Make sure you go all the way to your dog with the treat so your dog does not have to get up to reach the treat. Remind your dog that she is supposed to be staying by holding your palm up toward her face. After another brief pause, say "OK," bow, and back up. Be sure the release is crystal clear—how else will she know when it's OK to get up? When you release your dog, be boring. Stay was the fun part because she got treats. The release part means nothing happens. Yawn, snooze. Remember it is your job to help your dog win—early stays should last less than a second. Once she gets the idea, you can increase the length of time relatively quickly, but start with "micro-stays," and she will get the idea amazingly fast.

Once she gets the hang of Stay, gradually increase the difficulty of:

- the *time* the dog is asked to stay

- the amount of *distractions* around the dog

- the *distance* between you and the dog

Be sure to change only one factor at a time—extra longs Stays should occur with you close by and where it's relatively quiet. Stays that occur in active, distracting areas should be right at your feet and for very short durations. The biggest challenge for your dog (and you as a trainer) is to get your dog to stay while he's super distracted—say the kids are playing ball in the back yard and King is chomping at the bit to go play too. This is the time to ask for a micro-stay, then release King and let him join in the fun. Try for much longer stays in the family room after a long play session.

Correct Breaks with Body Blocks: Once you begin to increase the amount of time she's supposed to stay, be sure to correct her the millisecond she starts to break, not after she's gotten up. Use visual signals so that your dog understands you—throw your arms out to the side to block either side of you and move forward in a blocking motion at the instant she first begins to get up. I call this a Body Block, and I learned to do it by watching Border collies herd sheep and cattle. These relatively small dogs control the actions of huge animals primarily by blocking their forward motion with their bodies. Dogs and wolves do the same thing to each other: I am convinced that pack leader canids control the behavior of others mostly by controlling space. Watch a dominant dog or wolf—they don't push or pull subordinates around, they simply restrict their access to the environment by controlling the space around them.

Once you get the hang of it, it is incredibly gratifying to realize that you can control the behavior of your dog without ever touching her. What power! And your dog will love you for it, because you're not jerking at a leash or grabbing for his collar. Finally, you're talking dog! If you are late, don't worry, there's always next time. If you have trouble, you might try backing up a bit more, it helps to have some room to maneuver when you're doing this. If your dog is right at your feet it's too hard to move sideways to block him in time. By the time you react she's past you already!

Remember to say "Stay" only once, don't repeat yourself verbally. Herd her back in position with your legs, or lure her back where she started, but don't repeat "Stay." Otherwise, your dog will think it was acceptable that she broke and now you are starting over again. Then release her just as soon as she looks settled.

Don't expect too much of your dog. Practice in lots of very short sessions, scattered throughout the day. It takes a lot of work to get a dog to stay through high level distractions, but dogs understand the concept quite quickly. Older dogs can realistically be asked to "Lie Down" and "stay" five feet from their owners in a quiet room (while you watch TV or read) for an hour after only a month of training. Staying put while watching other dogs play is something else, however. Save that for the Advanced Dog Training book!

As you progress, slowly increase the length of the stay or the intensity of the distractions, but remember not to ask the dog to do a stay that's too far over his head—this is only the beginning of stay training, after all. A ten second stay with distractions is very hard for some dogs, while a minute long stay with nothing else going on (except you holding the dinner bowl) is pretty easy for adults, although still challenging for young pups of five months or so. While your dog is staying it is helpful if you frequently come to him, give him a treat, remind him with the visual signal that he should be staying, and praise him so he knows he is doing it right. Dogs who get treats while staying often develop such solid stays that they prefer to remain there even after you have given the release.

Block his attempts to get up from "Stay" with a Body Block, remembering not to repeat any verbal signal while you pantomime him back into place by herding him backwards an then visually signaling Sit. Release him when he settles down, not when he looks about to spring! Integrate surprise "Stays" into your day; before allowing him to go outside, on your way to the car, or during ball play. He will begin to anticipate wonderful things for being such a good dog.

"OK"

Be sure that you always verbally release your dog after "Stay," "Off" or "Wait" with a *release signal.* This is as important as the initial command, because it teaches her to continue a behavior until you signal her to do something else. If you don't say "OK," your dog will carefully watch for a visual signal that is associated with your "Good dog" and thus use some movement you don't even know that you're making as a release. Chances are you won't know what it is, and you and your dog will miscommunication about it.

Come

Practice Come … *always!!* Be sure that you call your dog often to come to you and *immediately release* him to go do something fun. Teach your dog that when you call him to come, something great will happen. Play hide and seek, play chase games, play "round robin" come games with your family, etc. Don't overdo this during one session. Two to four "Come" signals in one session is more than enough. Many sessions should contain only one or two "Come!" commands so that your dog doesn't get bored.

If you call your dog to come and he doesn't respond, you must *insure* that he does. You don't have to administer some monumental correction…just be sure that if you say "Lassie, Come!," she never gets away with *ignoring* you. This would be a great time to review the section on Come training in Chapter One!

Sit, Lie Down, and Stand

By now, "Sits" should primarily be rewarded with toys, releases, getting his dinner, etc. instead of treats. The exception is when he is very distracted, and sitting and listening is very hard for him. Even with few distractions, "Sit" is always easier than "Lie Down," so don't hesitate to give your dog more visual help with "Lie Down." Be sure not to *always* ask your dog to "Sit, Lie Down and Stand" in that order: sometimes just ask for a "Sit," and sometimes ask your dog to "Lie Down" from a stand (this is harder for them than from a "Sit," so help them do it right). Some catch on right away, while others take awhile to figure it out. Help them by being consistent with your signals. Take the time now to insure that all the family members are giving consistent verbal and visual signals, and that Fido doesn't get a treat each and every time he sits anymore.

Body Blocks in Heeling

Practice lots of right and left hand turns this week, concentrating on perfecting your timing with body blocks. Don't let this new move intimidate you! Avoid walking in a boring, straight line by zigzagging a lot. When you turn left, or *into* your dog, stride boldly around Chester in a half circle so that your body blocks him from moving ahead of you. Meanwhile, smooch, click or talk happy talk to encourage him to keep moving with you. As always, give him treats for being in the right position. If you find yourself running into your dog, it's because you turned when he was already too far ahead, so next time do it when he's farther back.

When you turn right, slightly bend your knees, slap your left leg and talk to keep his attention on you. Remember, he'll have to speed up to stay with you, so encourage him with your voice and quick little steps. The main goal for this week is to teach Chester that it's fun to pay attention to you, and that he never knows which way you're going to go. The point of your body blocks is to teach him that he should pay attention to you and not forge ahead. Meanwhile, he gets lots and lots of goodies (treats, happy talk, squeaky noises, etc.) from you when he stays by your left side. So: change direction, change your pace, turn around toward the left to discourage forging ahead, click, smooch, be silly and above all, keep your sessions short, playful and upbeat!

Chapter 4

Play, Training, and Play Training

PLAY AS TRAINING, TRAINING AS PLAY

This is a great time to concentrate on combining your training with play. Your dogs will know some exercises well enough for you to ask for a quick "Sit," or a short "Stay" as a prelude to a good game. Without question, the best way to train your dog is to incorporate obedience exercises into play sessions. Then your dog will do what you ask willingly because she wants to, rather than grudgingly because you made her. Think of how easy it was to accept the rules of some game you learned as a child. The game was fun, you accepted the rules as part of the game and didn't think twice about them. Compare that with your reactions to some proclamation made by your parents that came out of the blue. Imagine how you felt in each circumstance, and then ask yourself which attitude you want to deal with in your dog. Hummm. Think carefully.

> *"Without question, the best way to train your dog is to incorporate obedience exercises into play sessions."*

Here is an example of part of a "Day in the Life" of 14 week-old Kit in combined play and training sessions:

- Open crate while saying "Kit, Come!"; greet by rubbing on chest. Slap leg to keep her attention on you, walk to door, ask Kit to "Wait."

- Open door and say "OK." You go out first, trot outside with her to her potty place, say "Go Pee." Praise her for going, then clap and run away.

- As she runs to you, say "Kit, Come!" and continue running. Hide behind the house!

43

- When she finds you, giggle and run the other way, saying "Kit, Come!" as she changes direction to keep up with you. Give a little food reward when she gets to you.

- Pick up the ball, wave it in front of her face, throw it 4 feet, clapping and backing up when she picks it up.

- Take it from her, saying "Drop," then instantly give it back, saying "Take It." Say "Drop" again, then throw the ball again.

- Run away to the door, call "Kit, Come!" while clapping. Run into the house as she runs toward you and continue into the kitchen by her dinner bowl.

- Ask her to "Sit, Lie Down, Sit and Lie Down" for her dinner.

- Take her outside as soon as she's done, say "Go Pee" (or whatever!). Praise when she potties, then call her to come. As soon as she does, ask for a "Sit."

- Immediately throw a ball or stick after she sits. Take her on walk. Twice during the walk, while she's busy sniffing, clap your hands and run fast away from her—run far enough away so that she has to work to catch up with you.

- Praise with "Goooood" as she runs toward you, chuck her under the chin and then continue walking in another direction.

Once you're in the habit, this is much harder to write down than it is to do. Clearly the details may not fit your situation; my goal is to illustrate how *obedience* can be part of your dog's life. Listening to you should be the gateway to doing fun things, rather than some boring task imposed on your dog once a day. Right now, think through your daily interactions with your dog, and consciously design a day that incorporates training and play as part and parcel of the same thing. Once you get into the habit, you won't have to do it consciously…you'll just do it! I find puppies easier and easier to raise each time I get one now, simply because I'm learning more and more about how to incorporate training into my daily routine.

AVOIDING PLAY-RELATED PROBLEMS

How you play with your dog (and how you don't play with your dog) makes a big difference in how your dog behaves the rest of the time. Most dogs arrive having had lots of experience playing with their litter mates, and they assume you want to play the same way. But be careful, because certain types of play can lead to serious problems later on in life.

Play Mouthing and Biting. Puppies play together by grabbing each other with their mouths, and learn that hard bites result in yips of pain from offended playmates, who don't seem to want to play any more. Puppies quickly learn to *inhibit* their bites if they want to keep playing. This is an excellent lesson for all dogs to learn. The more fine-motor skills dogs have with their mouths, the less likely they are to bite too hard in a panic when a harmless snap would have done the job. However, a play bite that doesn't bother another dog may be too hard for us delicate human types. It is up to you to teach your dog that you are *not* like her litter-mates. You don't have a lovely coat of fur, nor do you have tough dog skin.

Since you can't assume dogs arrive understanding that we humans are so delicate, you must go out of your way to teach them. I like to teach *bite inhibition* first, so that my pups learn to be extra careful with their mouths around my skin. Later I change the rules and teach them not to mouth on me at all. Begin this process simply by yelping in pain when the dog puts any pressure on you with her teeth. Your yelp must be *very loud and abrupt*, bursting into the air like a popped balloon. The closest phonetic equivalent I can find is "AWRP!" If done correctly, it will elicit a *startle response*. Your pup will stop and look at you in shock for a brief second. During that microsecond pause, you *immediately* grab the closest toy and encourage her to mouth on it, not you.

If you do this right, she will understand that she hurt you, learn to be extra careful of her mouth around those tender humans and go directly to a toy instead of your forearm. When you really think about, there is little more cherished than a dog who is dependable with her mouth, and can be counted on to not hurt anything, ever, with her teeth. So don't skip this phase, even if you're sure Katie would never ever bite you. Give her a break. She's a dog. She has teeth and nothing else to defend herself. So unless she's hired her own attorney, help her learn finesse with her mouth so you can brag about her soft mouth to your grandchildren.

What if Spot gets worse? If King does not respond to your yelps by stopping (even just for a millisecond), then don't continue to repeat your cries. I've seen some older dogs get more excited than before by those fun noises their humans were making, and get even more vigorous in their play mouthing. I just talked to a couple who said they were shocked when it worked on a pup they were babysitting. It had always made their dog worse and they couldn't imagine it working! I'd guess it works on over 95% of the dogs I've seen, but who knows which ones those will be. If you can't get a yelp to work, then simply walk away in a huff. Let him know that mouthy play results in no play at all. Be very melodramatic here—say *Well!* like Jack Benny and leave in disgust. Your dog should be looking at you in shock, wondering what he did to get you to stop playing. If King just grabs ahold of your pants as you try to leave then you'll have to correct him with a gruff "No" or a physical correction (see Chapter 5).

What about Kids? Young kids don't seem to yelp like young puppies—they're usually too quiet to have the right effect and the dog ends up even more excited and more mouthy. It does seem to help a lot to have an adult do the yelping for the child. I originally tried this when a young female dog started playing too rough with four week old puppies. The dam and I both watched, getting more and more nervous as young Kit got rougher and rougher with the pups. Finally, I yelped as if I'd been hurt, and Kit leaped up and looked startled. I monitored her play for the next two sessions, yelping when I thought she was too rough and the pups looked big-eyed. After that she was always very gentle to pups, acting like an loving young aunt to someone's else babies.

Help your Dog Play Right. Be sure not to inadvertently teach your dog to be especially mouthy. Teaching inappropriate play is regrettably very easy to do. Any type of play that involves you grabbing at your dog with your hands will encourage him to use his mouth to grab you back. After all, how is that different from him biting you? If you grab and hold on with your hands, why shouldn't he do that to you with his mouth? I don't think dogs make *hand vs. mouth* distinctions. As a matter of fact, I suspect they think we are developmentally disabled, and make up for the lack of *real* muzzles with our paws.

The *worst* possible thing you can do is to play by slapping the pup on the side of the face with alternating hands. This action *begs* him to try to snap, nip or bite at you. Don't get mad at the dog when he snaps at your two-year-old child later on. I just saw a client who's sweet, friendly dog, after three years of vigorous wrestle and face slapping play, bit her human playmate severely in the face and neck during a play session. It happens, honest. To nice dogs and nice people. Don't let it happen to you.

> ### *"Any type of play that involves you grabbing at your dog with your hands will encourage her to use her mouth to grab you back."*

Recall from Chapter 3 how wrestle play can cause trouble. Litter mates and siblings play rough and tumble—pack leaders either don't play or *always* win, and you simply are not going to know how your dog defines "winning" when you're in a heap on the rug, giggling. So what do you do? Easy…there are lots of games to play with your dog, many of them are mentally challenging as well as physical. An ideal way to combine play and exercise in a constructive way is to teach your dog to fetch.

Teaching Lady to Fetch
Dogs Fetch, People Throw! The first rules are simple to explain, but a little harder to do: Never fetch *for* your dog, and never play chase games where you chase your dog around the yard. Chasing your dog will destroy any chance you have of getting her to come when called. She will try desperately hard to get you to chase her when she has the ball, because *dogs love to play tag*. Once she's gotten you started, you'll have a *terrible* time getting her to bring the ball back to you.

Fetch Training. Start by waving the ball in front of your dog's face—it's probably the movement that interests her, more than the object. When Lady is fixated on the ball, throw it only a few feet away. Pray that Lady trots over and puts her mouth around it. If she does, softly clap your hands and move backward, bending over and backing up to encourage her to come to you. If she comes part way with the ball, and then stops and tries to get you to chase her, back up again, clapping and running *away* from her, continuing to lure her toward you.

If she does bring the ball you must *instantly throw it!* Don't stand there like a fool, hoarding the ball to your bosom and say "Goooood Dog." Who cares! You talk to her all the time, right? She *wants the ball*, and you've got it! If you don't throw it, then you're *hoarding* it, and why should she bring it back next time?

"Teaching your dog to fetch is an ideal way to combine training, play and exercise."

Most young dogs will only fetch a few times, so don't be discouraged if she fetches only twice and then stops. (She'll probably be much more reliable in the house too. This is common, so expect only one or two fetches outside in early training.) Just consistently teach her that if she brings you the ball, you'll either give it back to her or throw it. If she brings it back three times, and then lies down with it, either walk away or lure her to you with a second ball. Try next time to end before she does, so you always stop when she wants more.

If she comes all the way up to you but won't give you the ball, either continually turn away from her with folded arms (she might drop it) or take it out of her mouth and then *instantly* throw it. You can also try to lure her into opening her mouth (and dropping the ball she has) by waving a second ball right in front of her nose. As she drops the first one say "Drop," and remember to throw it the microsecond she drops it for you.

But if Lady doesn't even pick up the ball, then go back to step one and try to entice her to mouth the ball by *waving* it in front of her face. If she even looks at it, snatch it away a few times and giggle. Nothing like the old "hard to get" game —works like a charm on dogs as well as humans! After a few times, when she seems really eager, *give it to her* and say "Goooood Dog." After a few sessions of this, most dogs learn that there's a neat game here, and begin to play by picking up the ball. You can also stuff food inside a hollow toy to increase motivation.

Gradually work up to throwing the ball more often, but be patient. Lots of six month old dogs will only fetch three to four times in a row (especially if outside), although some obsessive retriever-types will exhaust you *long* before you tire them out—no matter how young they are! It took about six months for my Border collie Luke to become insane about the tennis ball—he would only fetch once or twice at six months, then would look bored. Now he stops only from lack of oxygen, and is so obsessed with the ball he insists on keeping it in his mouth while he pants in an exhausted heap in the snow.

Summary. The key to teaching Fetch is to avoid teaching her to play "Tag...I'm it!"

with you. Rather, move *away* from her and play "hard to get." Dogs seem to perceive tag as a great game, and quickly learn to play *your* way. Be sure to take a *devil may care* attitude; this is a game after all. You can't force a dog to fetch playfully, so let her decide what to do next. Just be ready to:

- *encourage* the right response (by running backward as she moves toward you)

- *reward* the right response (by *instantly* throwing the ball or handing it back to her if she gives it to you)

- *ignore* her attempts to get you to play tag.

And just a word of caution: Be sure to warm your dog up carefully *before* playing demanding, difficult catch games, and don't set a young dog up to do too much jumping and twisting—it's hard on them and can cause serious injuries. If playing frisbee, be sure to use a soft, made-for-dogs frisbee; hard standard ones have broken far too many teeth already. Many veterinarians advise against playing canine frisbee, because dogs can injure themselves so badly landing wrong from their impressive leaps to catch the disc. Talk to your veterinarians about frisbee play if you are considering it; stick to ball play if you're conservative.

Tug Of War

This type of play is controversial, with some people advising you to never, ever play tug, and others saying why not? The reasons given for not playing tug of war revolve around the problem of bite inhibition and dominance. After all, here you are teaching your dog to bite down as hard as he can, and use the full power of his head, jaws, and neck to get what he wants. Does this mean that Duke will translate tugging into biting you or your kids later on?

Got me. There's no research out there to guide us. I certainly see lots of dogs who play tug of war and have never gotten in trouble with their teeth. On the other hand, you are encouraging exactly the type of behavior that causes trouble in other contexts.

I don't play tug with my dogs, but you should make your own decision. I would never play tug of war with a dog you've had any aggression problems with, or if you have young children. You have to decide as a family how to handle this, because dogs love to play tug, and so do many of their humans. If you really want to play tug games, then only do so under the following conditions:

- Allow tug games only if all the humans of the family can start them and then stop them by quietly saying "Drop."
- Always end up with you, the human, walking away with the tug toy.
  (Apparently in canid society whoever ends up with the tug toy also ends up with their social status uplifted (they won, right?).

So if you must play tug, don't end by giving the dog the toy and going to read the paper. Take the toy away, put it up, out of reach and keep it stored until you want to play tug again.

Tricks and Games

Don't think you have to restrict your play to Fetch and Come games. Teach your dog lots of silly tricks (see the book list in Chapter Six). Learn to train your dog to track or do Agility. Teach Spot to play Hide and Seek in the house. Teach Ginger to "Go Find" five different toys. Then you can watch the movie while she searches the house for the Kong that you hid.

Just remember that dogs need mental as well as physical exercise, and I think they like to play with their minds as well as their bodies, just like us. No wonder we get along so well.

Teaching a "Real" Heel Like a Game

Why Bother? I didn't always teach my dogs to heel close to my left leg, since I live in the country and have dogs who reliably come when called and lie down when told. But now I do, because in spite of myself I kept landing in one of two situations: either I simply need to know exactly where my dogs are for their own safety, (visits to the city, visits to the vet, at dog class—where not *all* dogs are friendly, etc.) or I needed to begin something with my dogs in a way that reminds them exactly *who* Alpha bitch really is!

Sheep herding is a good example of why heel is so important, although I'll grant that shepherding is not exactly sweeping the country as a leisure activity. But bear with me, there's a method to my madness.

My dogs compete in herding trials where they begin by running 100 to 300 yards away from me, then maintain mental contact with me while taking charge of a group of flighty, uncooperative sheep. Asking a keyed up dog who's running 20 miles an hour, 300 yards away from you to "Lie Down" while chasing after prey takes a certain amount of *mutual respect*. I have learned to start off right by insisting that my dog stay heeling by my side while we walk out onto the course—reminding Lassie that although we are in this together, I am Chairman of the Board. If she did run out ahead of me, she would perceive herself as the leader (well, she was in the lead, wasn't she?). You don't need to be a sheep dog competitor to be glad you taught your dog to heel. It'll come in handy, believe me.

Say, for example that you've just driven to the park. You know there will be other playful dogs there, and lots of squirrels waiting to tease your dog as soon as you get out of the car. You want Spot to have a good time, but you're not totally certain Spot will stop playing with his friends when you're ready to go. You could either let Spot knock you over, lunging out of the car before you've even undone your seat belt, or you could tell Spot to "Wait," release him to your feet, say "Sit" instantly and then "Heel" for twenty feet toward his friends. Then you release him with a happy "OK," having made the following points: 1) Access to playtime comes through you—("boy is heel a great thing to do, I always get to play when I do it!") and 2) You are in charge, and when you call "Come" it is coming from Alpha him or herself.

Keep in mind that there is nothing equivalent to "heel" in a wolf or dog pack. "Sit" is easy to teach, because we don't really have to teach dogs to sit, just to do it when we ask. Heel, on the other hand, isn't something dogs normally do, so be understanding of your dog's resistance to learn a perfect heel in a few weeks. After all, "Heel" could be defined by dogs (and no doubt is by many) as: "Walk beside your human at an intolerably slow pace ignoring all interesting things." Wow, bet they can't wait to learn that! But if you make it into a fun, new game and don't over do it, your dog will want to play.

Starting Heel with Treats. You've already begun if you've done the "following" exercises in the last chapter. "Heel" is just a more precise version of "follow." Start the same way, but this time, only reward your dog if she is in the exact position you have defined as "Heel." She should be right beside your left leg, but don't treat her if her head is in *front* of your leg. Be sure she is beside or behind you so that you don't teach her to stay out in front. She'll want to do this enough on her own without you encouraging it, and if she's ahead of you, well, she's in the lead again, which is what you're trying to avoid!

Giving her treats for being in the right position means you'll probably give Misty 35 pieces of liver in a four minute exercise, so be prepared with lots of tiny tasty training treats. Be sure to have some in your hand as you walk. If you have to stop and get them out of your pocket you'll be too late.

> ### *The most common mistake that people make when heeling their dog is to miss reinforcing them when they're in the right position."*

Be Unpredictable! Again, do lots of quick turns and pace changes. If you turn right, or away from your dog, bend your knees a bit, pivot on your feet and pat your leg or wave a lure as you stride out of your turn. Dogs begin to love this—I'm amazed at how quickly most of them will watch for your turn and try to anticipate it.

Body Blocks in Heeling. During your crazy, unpredictable zigzagging, be sure to practice your "body blocks". When you turn left, be sure to do so before your dog gets ahead of you, turning in front of your dog so that he slows down and looks up at you. If your dog's head was beside or behind you, your action will simply block his forward motion, and cause him to pause a bit, look up at you as you move around in a circle, and tend to stay closer to your side. If you run into your dog, then he was too far ahead of you when you started, so turn right to get him behind you and try another left turn when he's not so far ahead of you. Work on your timing here: try to get him the treat either as you're turning or the instant that you straighten out. This move, a moving version of a body block, can help your dog learn a really stupendous heel.

Leashes. Leashes are your worst enemy when training a heel. If you pull your dog around with your leash he'll never learn what heel means. Do all the exercises with a loose leash, only using the leash as a safety net. Remember that every time you pull slowly on the leash your dog will want to pull back. So if you do have to use your leash, give a quick gentle snap rather than a slow pull to avoid being a wagon for your Malamute to haul through the neighborhood. You won't need a leash except as a safety net if you've found a lure that is competitive with those interesting smells on the ground. Tiny food treats work for most dogs, squeaky toys drive some terriers wild and some dogs will do anything if you lure them with a tennis ball. Experiment to see what works best for your dog.

Summary. "Heel" can either mean "walk slowly beside your human at the pace of an elderly tortoise ignoring all interesting things" *or* it can be a fun game that you play with your dog. You make it a game by rewarding her *every time* that she is beside your left leg and the leash is loose. That means you need to pay attention…just like your dog! Be obsessive about only doing this for short periods of time (five to ten seconds at first, no longer than a minute after a week). Both you and your dog will have trouble concentrating for too much longer than that at first.

EXERCISES

By now you have introduced many new signals to your dog: "Come, Sit, Lie Down, Stand, Stay, Wait, Off, No, Good, OK and (pre)Heel." That's *a lot* to learn when you think about it! Now your job is to *continue* to:

- Wean your dog from *food* as a lure and a reinforcement for the things he knows well by now. Use praise, play, or just an interesting movement from you to reward her more, using food less and less. Keep using food generously for new exercises like "Heel," or listening and responding to you when there are lots of distractions.

- Begin to teach your dog to *listen*, as well as to watch—practice "disappearing the cue" by making your visual signal less obvious and saying the command first, before you move.

- Expand the *context* of the signal. Don't just do "Sits" in the kitchen…do them in the parking lot, the front yard, on a walk, etc. Otherwise, Chelsea will "Sit" in the kitchen, but nowhere else!

Sit, Off, Stand, and Wait

Easy to teach, aren't they? But don't overdo it, or your dog will get bored. Be sure to use these as a way for her to get something she wants, but don't bore her to death by doing them too often just because they work so well! However, end on something simple, like "Sit," after a difficult training session. Be sure *sitting on cue* has become part of your dog's daily routine.

Lie Down

"Lie Down" takes longer to teach than "Sit," so this may still need more actual training with lures from you for several more weeks. Lots of dogs really seem to dislike lying down on cue, so go out of your way to make "Lie Down" a ticket to get to play, go on walks, etc. Be sure their hips are flipped when they lie down, so that they are lying on one hip or another, not crouched in a Sphinx-like ready to spring posture that says "I'm going to get up any millisecond!"

Come

Ah, "Come"…What could be *more* important than "Come?" Are you still playing the "Come" game? Four to five times a day? I hope so, this is oh so important and simply takes time and energy on your part. Be sure to keep the following in mind:

- Running away from your dog is what gets most dogs to follow. Play bows are the second most likely movement to attract dogs toward you, so be sure to bend forward a bit when your dog looks at you.

- The right sounds are critical here: clapping, smooching, and making high repeated notes like "pup, pup, pup" work best.

- When your dog runs toward you, but then veers off two or three feet away from you, be sure to counter by zigging as they zag, preventing them from going by you because you keep moving the target. Play hard to get! It works with dogs too.

Heel

Work on heel in short, fun sessions. I'll ask for heel 5 to 10 times in a session, but only for a few seconds at first. Remember to be liberal about rewarding at first, so she can figure out the game!

Chapter 5

Trouble-Shooting

Lassie was an Actor: You know those wonderful dogs you see on TV or occasionally at the park, who do everything their owners ask, no matter what's going on? Chances are that didn't just happen. Someone spent years training that dog to listen so attentively, so don't despair if your dog doesn't. You may someday be one of the few people in the world lucky enough to get an "automatic" dog who does whatever you want, whenever you want it without years of training. If you get one, as I have with my Lassie and her father Luke, count your blessings. These dogs are one in a million. But most of the obedient dogs you see are listening and obeying because someone put in the time and effort for three or four years to train them. They had lots of set backs and frustrations. So, don't be discouraged if your dog isn't like that super star you saw in training class. Keep at it and enjoy the ride, remembering that stamina is as important in dog training as it is in everything else in life.

How to Handle Disobedience

So if your dog isn't perfect (if he is, you should be writing this book, not reading it!), what *do* you do when King completely ignores you in the park? What if Queenie is barking out the window at the squirrel from hell and you're on the phone with your mother-in-law? This chapter will help you have a plan for what to do if your dog doesn't listen, and presents some ideas on preventing and inhibiting problem behavior like jumping up and barking.

Here are some questions you should ask yourself whenever your dog doesn't do what you've asked:

Help or Authority?

Help Your Dog by being Clear: Ask yourself if your dog needs your *help* or needs a little *authority*. Dogs need help if they don't understand the signal—this includes either a sloppy cue from you or asking him to do something in a *new context*. Sloppy cues are easy to give if you're not sure what the relevant cue is to your dog. Do you say "Sit" but cock your head most of the time when you say it? Be sure you know which signal your dog is attending to—it may not be the one you think. King may be watching your head while you're focusing on the word "Sit." This happens particularly often when you have company or are out visiting. Because the context has changed, *you* change how you behave, and inadvertently drop out the cue he was looking for.

"Remember that every time you change the context of the signal, your dog may be confused."

Help Your Dog in New Contexts: Putting the dog in a new context requires that you *help* him, not correct him. If, for example, you've never asked Prince to "Sit" beside a busy road, and he's nervous about the noise, he needs your help, not a correction if he doesn't "Sit." Don't fuss over him, but get his attention with something he likes, ask for a "Sit," and then reward him for a correct response. If you have to gently ease him into a sit physically, go ahead and do it, all the while letting him know he's a good dog and that you're pleased with him, mind boggled though he may be. Remember that every time you change the context of the signal, your dog may be confused, so give him the benefit of the doubt.

Guard against getting irritated and thinking: "I *know* he know's this, he's just being disobedient." When did you last do something right every single time after you did it right just once? Imagine you're learning tennis, and you hit a couple of nice serves for the first time. Then your partner changes and your serve falls apart. Should your coach slap your face? He *knows* you *know* it, after all.

Context changes are part of training. It is your job to understand when the context changes and when it doesn't. The only general rule of thumb I can give you is that it takes very, *very* little change to throw off a dog at first, or a human for that matter. Think about "dress rehearsals" and how wearing different clothes completely throws even professional actors for a loop the first time they practice in them. We don't generalize from one context to another either, so be aware that "Sit" in the kitchen and "Sit" at the park are simply not the same thing at first, and help her work through all the different situations of life.

Be Authoritative When Necessary: On the other hand, what if nothing has changed and you know you're being clear? It happens to all of us: sometimes our dogs are just ignoring us because, well, they'd rather ignore us. I don't know if dogs consciously test us to see what they can get away with, but they certainly learn when they can and can't act like we're not there. In that case, a no-nonsense kind of authority is what's needed. Read on.

It's Not Over 'Til It's Over: If you are *sure* your dog understands exactly what you want, go directly to the Nike approach: "Just do it." What matters here is how the "exercise" ends, not how long it takes to get there. Great trainers have tremendous stamina, and know that even though it might take five minutes to get what they want, what mattered was ending the right way.

You need to get your dog to comply with your command relatively quickly and with little fuss, but don't panic and get angry and rushed. It is best to not repeat yourself with an older dog. Rather, say it once and then ask again *visually.* Be aware of how your body posture and visual signals effect your dog's behavior. For example, to enforce a signal like "Sit," it is often helpful to move forward toward the dog, imposing your authority as it were (be sure you are standing up straight, who listens to a slumper!) In contrast, some dogs lie down more easily if you give them a little room and actually move back a step or two. If your dog is distracted by some kids across the road and ignores your "Sit," you might move your body between your dog and the kids before repeating the signal visually.

If you are sure your dog understood, but is still ignoring you, you might say his name in a low voice. I know that dozens of books tell you never to use your dog's name as a correction, but I like the idea of communicating the following to the dog: "Excuse me, but you know what you need to do and I'm not here to always fix your mistakes for you! Bring your attention *back* to me and make your own decision about what needs to be done!" This is especially helpful for people like me who are always tying to "fix" things— you know, us helper types who want to save the world, starting with our dogs! I'm impressed with how often a dog will act oblivious to you until you say his name in a low, displeased voice. "Oh!" they seem to say, "yes, of course, I was just getting to it!" You can also say "Ah!" or "No" in a low, gruff voice to let them know that what they are doing is wrong. Remember that *any sound* that you would use here as a correction should be low pitched and a little growly. *Loud* is not necessary, but low and *authoritative* is.

When verbal signals, visual signals, and body posture changes don't work (all those should occur a lot faster than you can read them here!), then physically place your dog. Don't be *mad* or think of this as a punishment…just do it. The message you are conveying should be: "If I say sit, you will end up sitting. Period. Simple. No big deal, just truth." Once done, don't get all silly over your dog and tell him what an angel he was. He wasn't, he was a jerk, so show him what he would've gotten *if* he'd been good—and then take it away. This is a great opportunity for your dog to learn something, so ask again *and then instantly reward a good response* if you get it.

One summer I taught myself to respond to my dog Luke's disobedience while sheep herding by saying: "Oh good, a training opportunity." That change in my behavior probably had *more* effect on his behavior than any other one thing I've ever done. Try it with your dog; (maybe even with your family??). If you find yourself not getting anywhere, don't continue practicing the exercise over and over. We all have bad days, and sometimes we are just better off not practicing the piano that day.

Who's in Charge Here: If you're having trouble with your dog attending to you, ask yourself if you need to go back and work on the basic relationship between you and your dog. He needs to learn that you are interesting *and* important. Work on motivating him to be glad he sat when you asked, because it's associated with games, a release to go sniff, chest rubs, liver treats or whatever he wants that second. Teaching your dog to pay attention to you is the name of the game, and once you have that solved, you're darned near done. If King continues to turn his head away from you, pretend he doesn't hear you, or sniff the ground while you repeat "Sit Sit Sit Sit" like a cuckoo clock, then you need to work on some basics.

Does he get free petting all the time, just for being cute, or does he have to earn it? Sure you should pet your dog, but not because he demanded it, but because he earned it. Are you integrating obedience into play, and into his daily routine? If you call "Come!" *and he does,* what happens? Do you shut him in the crate? Clip his nails? Pet him on the head when he clearly doesn't want you to? Or toss his ball, let him go run around free in the yard, or go see that dog next door?

Ask yourself, is he the initiator or are you? Who decides what to do when? In other words, who's the leader—you or your dog? You must become the *window through which he finds both joy and security,* (rather than the wet blanket who always ruins the fun). Nor do you want to be the follower who looks to your dog to decide what to do. If any of this sounds unfamiliar, go back and re-read Chapter Three.

"Sure you should pet your dog, not because he demanded it, but because he earned it..."

Here's a Specific Example of How to Handle an Obedience Problem:

After months of playing the "Come" game with your dog, you call "Come!" at the park. You, good student that you are, say his name first, clearly say "Come" in a rising tone, clap your hands and whistle short, repeated rising notes. Who could not come to that? Apparently your dog Oscar, who wants to go say hello to a gang of canine street toughs. He stops at the sound of your voice, looks at you, looks at his erstwhile new friends, looks at you, and turn and trots toward a life of canine crime. Now what?

First off, I would not keep calling "Come!" I would say "Hey! or No!" or his name in a low, gruff voice, and then trot after him, talking in low nasty grumbles all the while ("your mother eats kitty litter"—no wait, that would be a compliment to a dog). I like to say silly things because it cheers me up, but it doesn't matter what you say, just sound gruff and grumbly. If possible I'd throw something in front of him to stop his forward progress. If not, when I got to him, I would physically block him, perhaps throw something now and say (gruffly) "No!" again.

Now go right back into the game—call him to come again sweetly as if nothing has happened, and make him oh so happy he did. If at all possible, let him have what it was he wanted in the first place. If not, substitute something you *know* he adores, like a chase game or fetching a bird wing. It's very helpful to work through every problem as it happens. In this example, I'd ask him to come five more times in a similar context, except I'd stack the deck on my side so that he was closer, and thus more likely to come the first time. Then I'd insure he was really truly glad he came by playing chase, releasing back to play with the other dogs and/or going on a long, fun walk. The key is to use a correction that prevents him from being rewarded when he's disobedient, and reminds him that it's in his best interest to do what you ask. The following section elaborates on giving corrections that *instruct* rather than punish.

Corrections

Learning how to give humane, effective corrections takes some initial effort and lots of practice. Most of us seem to either correct too little, so that the dog thinks we are playing, or too much, so that he becomes defensively aggressive. Corrections should not be punishment oriented; rather they should be designed to *stop* the dog from doing something inappropriate, and encourage him to do what is right.

Most corrections should be *remote*, meaning that they occur independently of you being near the dog. He does not need to know that they come from you. If King discovers that every time he chews on a electric cord something scary crashes to the ground in front of him, then he'll decide not to do it anymore, *whether you're in the room or not.* I don't hesitate to stop a dog from doing something I don't think is right by throwing something—an empty pop can with coins in it (tapped shut), a bean bag, a paper back book, etc. Anything to startle him as he is doing something wrong that startles him right there and then. If you just yell "No!" and then run toward your dog to stop him, he's learned two things:

- My owner doesn't like me doing this, so I'll do it when she can't stop me.

- My owner can be dangerous and untrustworthy. Perhaps she suffers from inbreeding.

So don't teach your dog to be afraid of you, teach your dog it's no fun to chew on the cord or lift your leg in the house. Say "No!" or "Ah!" *before* you throw something, and your dog will quickly learn to stop what he's doing and look up at the sound of your voice. Be sure to say "Good Dog" if your dog does stop what he's doing, and then redirect him so that he is doing something acceptable.

The ideal *remote* **correction is your voice,** since you always have it with you. Most importantly your voice, if used as a correction, needs to be low pitched. This is easier for men because their larynx's are designed differently than women's. Women's voice boxes tend to create high, squeaky notes when we try to get loud, which conveys the authority of a frightened mouse. So if your voice is not naturally low, practice speaking in a low voice, saying "No!" ten times at the stop light while driving to work. (I had to practice "Lie Down" too, since my voice would go up at herding dog trials when I was nervous!)

Combining Remote Corrections: If you say "No" right as you throw something, you are teaching your dog to pay attention to the sound of your voice. *Sound sensitive* dogs make it easy—they need no more than a gruff voice all by itself. All you need to do is to raise your voice a tiny bit and speak gruffly, and Ginger is on her back, groveling at pack leader (that's you). Other dogs aren't so sound sensitive, and the lowest, gruffest voice has virtually no effect whatsoever. These are the dogs that need your "No" connected with something else: a thrown pop can, a body block, or rarely, a leash snap. Remember that the sound should *bolt* out of your mouth! Sounds with an *instant rise time* (from silence to full power in no time at all) are inherently designed to get attention better than others...so don't let your verbal correction meander out of your mouth. Say it fast and firmly, and if at all possible, *without* anger. This works a lot better when you're rested and relaxed, so do what you can to avoid training when you're tired and harassed. That's what *time-outs* are for!

All corrections should be lightning fast! They should occur the millisecond your dog begins to misbehave, not when he's halfway through. If you can stop him as he initiates an act, you will prevent him from getting rewarded by completing the act, and you are halfway to eliminating it from his repertoire. You've already worked on this with "Stay," when you Body Blocked instantly upon seeing him *begin* to get up. Dog's reaction times are much faster than ours, and I suspect they think we move in slow motion. The quicker you are to react to your dog's behavior, the more control you'll have. This aspect of training is like a sport, in that you simply have to learn the "body work" necessary to combine your observations with your physical reactions. Just like tennis players who say that they can see the seam of the ball as it spins toward them (I can't see the *ball* half the time!), they are able to react *long before* the ball arrives. I'm confident that you can learn to respond to tiny, subtle intention movements that signal you *what he's about to do* before he does it.

Physical Corrections: Dogs rarely need strong physical corrections, as a matter of fact, most physical corrections that owners give their dogs are inappropriate, and can lead to defensive aggression from the dog or dogs who are afraid of their owners. But some dogs seem to be almost looking for you to set a boundary for them, and need to learn to be respectful. My preferred serious correction for a dog is not physical at all, at least if "physical" means that you touch them. Using a low, growly voice, I'll get right in front of a dog and start backing him up with assertive "Body Blocks". After backing the dog up a few strides, all the while grumbling and growling, I'll make a disgusted face (pull the corners of your mouth down) and let a loud "UGH!" burst out of my mouth while I turn my head sideways. It's as though the sound coming out of your mouth pushes your head to the side, almost like a recoil from a rifle. OK, OK, so I look crazy, but perhaps my dogs think so too, and what could be worse than an owner who's gone over the edge? I honestly don't know how dogs interpret these actions, but even Darwin wrote about universal expressions of disgust in dogs and humans, and I suspect that dogs understand that you're appalled when you exclaim "Ugh" and make a disgusted face.

The value of this "display" is that you aren't attacking your dog: you're not grabbing at her collar or running toward her so that she starts to run away from you. However, you're still giving her instant feedback that what she did was wrong. Sometimes I'll have a dog lie down and stay after I throw my little fit, just to cool things off and try to make the point that "this was serious stuff!"

Sometimes dogs really do need a physical correction, and on occasion I will give a dog a more traditional physical correction. But it's rare. If you think your dog might need one, you are better off talking to a professional trainer than trying to learn how from a book. A good physical correction is lightning fast, the dog is absolutely clear why it happened and it is over instantly. Pulling that off is an advanced skill, so avoid physical punishment until you are sure when it should be applied and exactly how to do it.

Jumping Up

Jumping up is a perfect example of the importance of timing in good corrections. It is a problem that is best solved by preventing the dog from getting rewarded by his action, and redirecting him into something appropriate. Timing is of the essence here—you must stop your dog on the way up, not after he's already jumped up, gotten paw contact, and is waiting for gravity to get him down again. Most people let their dog jump up, and then say "Down!" News flash—gravity will get them down eventually. Down is not the problem, *getting up* in the first place is the problem. The signals need to come sooner. (Secondly, using "Down" in this context just confuses your dog about the meaning of "Lie Down." Remember how important clear signals are). Think of any behavior as having a beginning, a middle and an end. You need to interrupt the behavior in the beginning or middle stages, because once an animal's gotten to the "end," he's been reinforced already. So use those *lightning fast* reflexes and stop him before his paws touch your leg.

> ### *"Down is not the problem...getting up in the first place is the problem."*

If Your Dog Jumps Up on You:
- Body Block your dog on his way up, just like you've learned to Body Block a break from "Stay." Simply move *into* him with your hip or leg, taking control of the space in front of him, and imposing your height over him. Immediately ask for a "Sit." Then, *and only then*, give him attention while he's sitting. If he's up as

soon as you start to bend over, block again, and try petting him quietly on his chest. This works best for me if I stay silent. Let your body do the talking.

- If the above doesn't work, try folding your arms and immediately turning 180 degrees away from your dog. I throw my nose in the air and follow it around, in a melodramatic display of rejection. Peek over your shoulder, and turn back toward him when he backs off. If he starts to jump again, you turn again. You may have to turn around 20 times at first, but most dogs learn after a few weeks that what they want goes away *unless they stay on the ground.* (What they want is your face, so they can give you an appropriately submissive canid greeting by licking your lips.) This works best on those dogs who leap in the air as if they *had* to get to your face, and the more you physically block them the higher they jump. I also like this method because your kids, friends, and neighbors can do it too. There is an occasional dog out there who hasn't read this chapter and will just climb on your back when you turn around. Either teach them to read or concentrate on teaching them what great things happen when all four paws are on the floor. If your dog is really "all over you" I'd suggest a private appointment with a professional trainer.

Barking Problems

Barking problems share the need for quick reactions. Most of us want our dogs to bark sometimes, but to stop when we ask. Notice I said "ask." Yelling "Shut Up" works about as well as barking back, because that's exactly what you're doing! Remember that barking is contagious, and loud noises from you will result in loud noises back from your dog.

Rather, teach your dog the word "Enough," by setting up a time when he is half-heartedly barking, saying "Enough," then instantly distracting him with something that overwhelms him into silence (food right by his nose, for example). Give him the food or other reward right away if he is quiet. Gradually expect him to be quiet for longer and longer before he gets a reward. After many repetitions of that, simply correct him if he begins to bark after the word "Enough" by instantly saying "Ah!" or "No!" and redirecting his behavior. This is not something that you can fix in a day—it will takes months of consistent work, but the resultant 15 years of golden quiet is well worth it! Like jumping up, instant feedback is what makes it work.

EXERCISES

Sit down and ask yourself how your dog is doing on each of the following:

Sit	**Come**
Stand	**Lie Down**
Stay	**Good Dog!**
Off	**Wait**
No, Ah, Or Hey!	**Leash Manners**

Be brutally honest—figure out what your dog is really good at, what is going slowly but in the right direction…and what isn't working at all. Experiment right now—ask your dog to do each of the above, and pay careful attention to his response in each of two contexts: *alone in the kitchen* or in the *front yard with distractions*. When your dog doesn't obey, ask yourself if he needs help or more authority. Work especially hard on your reaction time—exactly how much time goes by after you said "Lie Down" and Prince ignored you? How long did it take for you to do something else? One second? Two seconds? Three endless long eternal seconds? Play a game with yourself where you give you and your dog only *one second* to give a command and get a response, and notice how you hold your body as you do it. Do you stand straighter? Say it more quickly? Remember how you are speaking and moving and begin to incorporate *that* voice and *those* postures into your daily routine.

If you have access to a video camera, have a friend tape you and your dog. Then watch yourself carefully to see if your signals are consistent (remember to watch for visual signals as well as to listen for verbal ones). Play it back again and watch your dog's reactions—and your reactions to his behavior. See if you can watch in slow motion. It's amazing *how much* goes on inside just one second!

A reasonable set of expectations at this point would be a dog who…

Stops doing what he was doing when you say "No!" 90% of the time, who…

"Sits" *almost* all the time with no food lure, who…

"Lies Down" most of the time to a clear visual signal, who…

"Stays" up to 30 minutes when all is *quiet*, and 10 seconds in *chaos*, who…

"Comes" 85% of the time when called, who…

"Heels" beautifully for a *very* brief period of time (a perfect heel takes months—
if not years, that's why there are Intermediate and Advanced dog training classes!)

and, who…

"Waits" patiently at the door without bolting through first,

Doesn't jump up on visitors, and who…

Backs away from the popcorn you dropped when you say "Off!" from 5 feet away.

Not there yet? Don't worry, every dog is different. Some dogs take lots of time and patience with one signal, and no time at all on another. Age makes a huge difference here—6 month-old adolescent dogs simply do not have the emotional maturity to act like Rin Tin Tin yet. (But then neither do most grown up humans, so don't be too hard on him!) What matters here is your *objective* assessment of how your dog is doing. Feel proud about the progress you've made: I'm amazed at how frustrated we all can get because King didn't come away from a teasing squirrel, when he's come perfectly every time for the last three weeks. Rather we should celebrate how far we've come in the last month and objectively record that "coming from rude squirrels" is something we need to figure out how to proof through. Don't be discouraged at the low points, just develop a strategy and keep working. Great trainers have lots of stamina and understand that raising a young dog into a responsible adult takes years, not months. So celebrate the highs, consider how to fix what isn't working and bless your lucky stars that there are dogs in the world at all.

Chapter 6

Proofing

(...Or, Getting All This To Work When You Need it!)

You and your dog have hopefully learned a lot in the last several weeks. But there is still a lot of training ahead to insure that your dog reliably does what you ask, whenever you ask it. After all, getting Queenie to lie down when she wants to chase a squirrel is pretty advanced obedience. But that's when you need it most, so now is the time to start *pushing the limits* of your dog's obedience. Professional trainers think of the initial stages of training a "Sit" or "Lie Down" as a trivial process, easily accomplished in a day or two. The part that takes the work is the *proofing* stage, or teaching your dog to respond in different contexts and while distracted by other things. There are at least two aspects of *Proofing*:

Proofing Through Distractions

Each of us needs to thoughtfully teach our dogs to listen and obey when they are distracted by something else. Once you start to ask your dog to listen to you with lots of competing attractions (dogs playing, kids running, people at the door, etc.) you need to know exactly what you are going to do if your dog ignores you.

Set up the Situation Yourself: Go out of your way to set up the situation as specifically as possible. If, for example, Toto didn't listen to you when you called him to come away from playing with other pups, then set up the situation again, where you are closer this time and have a handful of liver for him when he does come. You must be aware that each context is different and needs to be handled separately. As your dog gets older he will start to generalize, but always be aware of the power of fixing the problem in the exact same context in which it occurred.

One the situation is repeated, but with you in control, be the *most fun* game in town: "If you Lie Down, you get to chase the ball;" "If you Stay, we can start your walk"; "If you Come, you can play some more." Just be sure to make the reward *immediate* upon completion of the correct response.

Don't Ask Questions: I hear a plaintive, questioning voice often when beginners say "Stay" in a way that says "I can't believe you will, would you please, maybe, please..."

Meanwhile the dog is up and moving before the word got out of their mouth. Practice saying "Stay" as if there's no chance your dog wouldn't. It's a statement of reality, period. Don't sound tentative, sound confident. Your dog will love it.

And When He Doesn't Listen? Non-compliance that is clearly the result of your dog ignoring you should be addressed with swift, yet non-judgmental action on your part—insuring a correct response. Your best response is a "neutral" one—quickly insure that your dog really does "Sit" by clearing your throat, using a visual signal, or tucking his rump in one smooth move so that he's sitting before he has time to think about it. Don't *punish* your dog at this stage. Just get the job done. On the other hand, if your dog quickly begins the correct response, but performs it slowly, don't rush her. You can work on the speed of completion later. Give her time to think if the signal is one that requires problem solving.

> *"Think of your signal as a statement, not a request.*
> *Non-compliance that is clearly the result of your dog ignoring*
> *you should be addressed with swift, yet non-judgmental action*
> *on your part—insuring a correct response."*

Proofing the Meaning of the Signal

The second aspect of *proofing* is teaching your dog what your signal really means. Gosh, I expect you thought you already did that. But this is much harder than most people realize.

Say, for example, that your dog sits almost every time you ask. Does that tell you what "Sit" means to your dog? No. Say "Sit" to most dogs who are already sitting, and they lie down, because to them, "Sit" means *Go down toward the ground.* Say "Sit" to a dog 15 feet away from you and they'll cheerfully trot toward you and "Sit" at your feet. As best I can tell, most dogs think "Sit" means: "Depress your body toward the ground, within 2 feet and in front of your owner." And after all, that is exactly what we taught her, right? So start working on "Sits" in the car, at the vet's, when she is lying down, if she is 5 feet from you, while watching a cat , etc.

Proof, or help your dog to define the signal *in every context* you can imagine, and that includes much more than just in different places. For example, if you ask her to "Sit" while she is lying down—she has to get up. That's a different context than asking her to "Sit" while standing. In that case, she has to go down to "Sit." Each of these movements are different actions, and I suspect that dogs learn actions more readily than they learn static postures. So think about the action you want, rather then focusing on the position itself, because that's how your dog will define it.

Write Out a Recipe: If you're having trouble with an exercise, try writing out a step-by-step plan of how you're going to accomplish it. For example, if right now your dog is good on "Heel" *only* if there are no distractions and you have a cookie, and you'd like a dog who trots off leash beside your left leg looking adoring into your eyes whether you have a treat or not, then sit down and write out a step-by-step plan of how you're going to get from here to there. There are about *100 steps* between those points, but most beginners try to turn it into two or three.

I always do better if I sit down about once a week and figure out where each dog is in her training, and what needs immediate work. This can help you to avoid spending your time on things already taught or expecting too much of your dog. It also comes in handy 6 to 12 months from now—you'll be amazed at how far you've come.

Dog Training is at Least Three Things...A Science, an Art, and a Sport.

The sport is your ability to observe subtle and quick actions of your dog and to instantly and accurately move your body and use your voice to *respond* to her behavior. It requires both excellent observational skills, (like ball players who can see the baseball as it flies toward them at 90 miles an hour), and quick reflexes, just like in any other sport.

The science is understanding the natural history of dogs and universal principles of learning.

The art is knowing when to help and when to correct. Not a month goes by that I don't realize I was interpreting a situation incorrectly: a dog was sincerely confused at something I never would've predicted, or a dog was playing me like a pack of cards and needed a correction rather than help.

Other Training Classes

Don't Stop Now! By all means take another class or continue private instruction. Classes vary at different training groups, but Dog's Best Friend's Intermediate and Advanced Classes are designed to proof your dog through distractions, to introduce off leash heeling, and to get your dog listening to you, off leash, up to 50 yards away. At the end of Advanced Classes your dog will "Stay" while other dogs play ball, come away from other dogs playing or eating liver, "Heel" nicely on and off leash, "Sit" or "Lie Down" instantly 10 to 20 feet away when you ask, and politely defer to you at the door. Well, maybe not *every single each and every* one of your dogs, but most of them!

Some of you will do best by repeating a class series. Don't hesitate to do this if you think your dog will profit from it. There are many factors to consider; the *age* of your dog, the breed, and their background before you started working with her. Many dogs (and their humans) would do much better to master the Beginning level exercises before moving on. Why not lay a good, solid foundation and let your dog be the star of the class the second time around!

Learn From Everyone: Go out of your way to learn all you can from *anyone* you can. There is no ultimate truth here, so go to other classes if you think you are ready to explore other methods and styles. You can't possibly develop your own style by watching only one person. They have their own style, and it evolved from watching scores of others. Everyone has something to teach you, even if it's how you don't want to train. Don't however, bounce willy nilly from trainer to trainer. Find someone you feel good about and learn their method thoroughly before you go on to someone else. I'd suggest sitting in on a class, without your dog, with the same instructor who would be teaching if you signed up. Avoid classes where you feel uncomfortable about any of the methods. By all means avoid classes that use a lot of physical corrections: if you see any yelling, hard leash corrections, or "stringing up" (holding a dog with all four paws off the ground by the leash and collar until they begin to pass out)…then *run,* don't walk out of there and say a prayer for the poor dogs who can't leave. You do not need to terrorize dogs to teach them something; as a matter of fact I'm not sure you can teach terrified dogs much of anything.

Other Types of Classes

After awhile, doing nothing with your dog but asking her to "Sit" or "Heel" gets pretty boring for all of us. Go out of your way to find some creative, fun classes for you and your dog! The following are just some of the classes that you and your dog might enjoy:

Agility Classes, where your dog runs a course of jumps, tunnels and balance beams. It's wonderful fun for dogs and owners alike, and is an excellent way to add a little confidence to a hesitant dog.

Trick Classes focus on teaching your dog to be a neighborhood star. What could be more fun than to teach your dog to listen to you by teaching movie tricks like "crawl," "go find Timmy in the burning barn," "pray," "roll over and play dead," or "balance a book on your head"! The sky's the limit, and the dogs love it.

Tracking Classes allow a dog to use her own natural abilities and follow a scent trail. Many dogs who *hate* classic obedience competition are great at this…(all dogs are better than humans, which seems to be good for their souls). These classes require active humans, since you have to lay trails and follow your dog over hill and dale.

Good Citizenship Classes grant certificates to dogs who have proven their manners in polite society: dogs who can be counted on to show friendly dispositions to strangers, stay when asked, not fuss over other dogs, etc.

Obedience Competition Classes are a very popular, traditional outlet for people who want to work with their dogs and gain titles. These competitions put a premium on precision, are highly competitive, and great fun for people who enjoy precision under pressure. Some dogs love them, others wilt.

The trick is to find what works best for you and your dog as a team. Don't worry if it takes awhile to find what "clicks"; you have years of fun ahead of you!

Perhaps the most important thing to keep in mind with training is that, like any relationship, you are never "done." You will always need to reinforce "Come" when your dog is distracted, though maybe only once a month. A solid "Stay," when that squirrel runs across the yard, will need polishing up every once in awhile. Queenie will need to be reminded that she is not a *sled dog* so she's not supposed to pull you horizontally through the air toward that handsome dog next door! Just incorporate these lessons into your daily life. Develop an awareness of what your dog is good at, stubborn about, and sincerely having trouble with—and act accordingly. Expect set-backs and bad days. Keep them in perspective and move on. I continue to be astounded at how willing and *forgiving* most of our dogs are (mine included!). Sometimes we even deserve them.

So tell them they're Olympic stars for a good heel, give them a gruff, verbal correction for pretending they didn't notice you told them to "Come," and celebrate a long, difficult, and *successful* "Stay." Then give them a sloppy kiss for me. Bless their furry little hearts.

READ, READ, READ! There is a wealth of information out there in print. Just be forewarned that there are dozens of techniques, and several very different philosophies— so some books will contradict each other. Right now, you're best off noticing that there are several universals in training. Pay attention to what all authors agree on and file away their disagreements for future consideration. Avoid skipping from one technique to another. Training takes time and experience, so you are better off trying the method that seems *most reasonable* for a good length of time, rather than listening to one author one week and another the next. But you can't lose by immersing yourself in the world of training and learning the basic principles of behavior. It's a skill like carpentry, neurosurgery, or cooking, and it takes *time and attention* to do well. Below is a bibliography of training books that I hope you will find helpful.

And don't limit yourself to books: check out some dog training videos and ask yourself what you like and don't like about the methods you see (One well advertised video, for example, illustrates methods that I really hate, but the trainer's timing is awesome.). If you've caught the bug and are really fascinated about learning more, contact local training organizations or check out doggie magazines for seminars in your area. There are some truly great workshops and seminars being run now, all over the country, by some excellent, knowledgeable people. Look for members of the Association of Pet Dog Trainers, a great group of people dedicated to increasing the professionalism of dog trainers all over the country.

Recommended Training Books

Behavior Problem Solving in Dogs
William Campbell, 1975, American Veterinary Publishers, Santa Barbara, CA.

Campbell "wrote the book" on using positive reinforcement to turn around problem behavior. Whether you have a problem or not, anyone interested in dog training will profit from reading this book.

The Cautious Canine: How to Help Dogs Conquer Their Fears.
Patricia B. McConnell, Ph.D., 1998, Dog's Best Friend, Ltd. Black Earth, WI

This 30 page booklet explains how to desensitize and counter-condition a dog out of his or her fears. This step-by-step approach clearly demonstrates how to change your dog's cautiousness, whether it's to strangers, veterinarians or garbage pails, into relaxed and happy anticipation.

Dog Training: Gentle Modern Methods
David Weston, 1991, Howell Book House, New York

This is a beautifully illustrated and reasonably priced book that covers the basics of using positive reinforcement to teach basic obedience commands. There's little text, but the photographs show clearly how you should use your body to lure and signal your dog. If you're looking to get a friend started out on the right paw, I'd suggest Weston's book for the photographs along with the book your reading for the text.

The Domestic Dog: its evolution, behavior and interactions with people
Ed. by James Serpell, 1995, Cambridge University Press, Cambridge, UK

Get this book if you want to really understand dog behavior. Written from an ethological perspective (the scientific study of animal behavior), this book is a series of chapters by different authors on most aspects of dog behavior. Except for a regrettably pallid chapter on a rich and multi-layered topic, communication in canids, it's excellent and very much worthwhile.

Don't Shoot the Dog
Karen Pryor, 1985, Bantam Books, New York

This little, easy to read paperback is the definitive word on how to use positive reinforcement and operant conditioning to influence the behavior of any animal, whether it's your dog or your spouse. Inexpensive, delightful to read, it's a wonderful addition in anyone's life. I like it so much I give it out in some of our Intermediate classes, even though it's about conditioning in general, not dog training per se.

Excel-erated Learning: Explaining in plain English how dogs learn and how best to teach them.
Pamela J. Reid, Ph.D., 1996, James and Kenneth Publishers, Oakland, CA.

Finally! A clear concise description of how operant and classic conditioning relate to our daily interactions with our dogs. This is a must for any serious student of animal training, all of Dog's Best Friends instructors have it and use it. Perhaps a bit elaborate for some dog owners, but hey, how many books teach you how to condition your human friends to blink on command?

Good Owners, Great Dogs
Brian Kilcommons, 1992, Warner Books, New York

A thorough, complete book on raising a dog, Brian has a loving, funny approach to dog training that I find delightful. I don't always agree with his methods—he tends to use a lot of leash corrections, but his general philosophy is positive and sensible.

How to Be Leader of the Pack and Have Your Dog Love You for It
Patricia B. McConnell, 1996, Dog's Best Friend, Black Earth, WI

You have this information already in Chapter 3. It is also available in a booklet form for people who need some coaching about letting Poochy know he is loved and cherished but not Leader of the Pack.

How to Teach a New Dog Old Tricks
Ian Dunbar, Ph.D., DVM, James & Kenneth Publishers, 2140 Shattuck Ave, #2406, Berkeley, CA

Without question, a great book on what is and what isn't important in the early stages of your pup's life. Contains invaluable information and methods on how to prevent problems with easy and fun techniques. Excellent philosophy on teaching rather than forcing. Highly recommended for dog owners of any age. Also, get his Sirius Puppy Training Video — it's great.

How to Teach your Old Dog New Tricks
Ted Baer, 1991, Barrons, Hauppage, New York

Need some ideas for tricks to teach Fido? Here's my favorite book about how to teach lots of fun tricks to amaze the neighborhood and keep Fido busy. I always wish I could take a month off when I read this book, so I could just spend a month teaching my dog to balance a book on her head!

In Tune With Your Dog
John Rogerson

Rogerson wows audiences with his creative and perceptive analysis of behavior problems in canids (not to mention his guitar playing!). Always worth reading, Rogerson has rewritten this older classic, which should be on every serious student's shelf.

People, Pooches and Problems
Job Michael Evans, 1991, Howell Book House, New York, NY

A beautifully written book about dog problems relating to status (or dominance) problems between people and their dogs. This is an excellent book for people who's dog is growling over toys, possessive about it's sleeping area, and just plain stubborn. I don't think he deals with fear related problems well, and since so much aggression is related to fear I advise caution about using these methods until the problem is diagnosed. But overall, a worthwhile book with many excellent ideas.

Puppy Primer
Brenda Scidmore and Patricia McConnell, 1996, Dog's Best Friend, Black Earth, WI

What can I say? I'm not very objective about this book, but I am very proud of it. The Puppy Primer covers important puppy-related issues such house training, play mouthing, crate training, etc., along with lots of good advice about training in general.

All Dog's Best Friend, Ltd. books can be ordered from our office at 608/767-2435 or FAX 608 767-3726. All of these books listed above, including mine, can be ordered from the ultimate dog book catalog: *Dogwise* at 800/776-2665 or FAX 509 662-7233.

ADDITIONAL TITLES BY
DR. PATRICIA McCONNELL

Puppy Primer

How to be Leader of the Pack
....and Have your Dog Love you for it

The Fastidious Feline
How to treat Litter Box Problems

The Cautious Canine
How to Help Dogs Conquer their Fears

I'll be Home Soon
How to Prevent and Treat Separation Anxiety

**For more information or to order these books,
contact Dog's Best Friend, Ltd. at
(608) 767-2435 or fax: (608) 767-3726**